María

FÁBULA DE LOS PERDIDOS

IF WE HAVE LOST OUR OLDEST TALES

Translated by Lorna Shaughnessy

General Editor: Lorna Shaughnessy
with contributions by
Olwen Rowe *and* Anthony Stanton

ARLEN
HOUSE

To: José

from: María !!

Happy Birthday

This publication was grant-aided by the Publications
Fund of **National University of Ireland, Galway**

Fábula de los perdidos was first published in Spanish
by Ediciones del Equilibrista, Mexico, 1990

First published in English translation in March 2006 by
Arlen House
PO Box 222,
Galway, Ireland
Phone/Fax: 00 353 86 8207617
Email: arlenhouse@gmail.com

ISBN 1–903631–19–X, *paperback*

Cover image: Aoife Casby
Typesetting: Arlen House
Printed by: Colourbooks, Dublin

CONTENTS

ACKNOWLEDGEMENTS

The translator would like to thank María Baranda for her generous responses to every query, Olwen Rowe for her insightful readings of many drafts of the translation as well as her authoritative notes, and Anthony Stanton for providing such an informative and perceptive context to the *Fábula* in his Preface.

The publisher wishes to acknowledge the support of the author María Baranda and her publisher Ediciones del Equilibrista, Mexico in the publication of this dual language edition of her poem.

Anthony Stanton

PREFACE

María Baranda started to write at a time when the traditional defining notions of generation, group and collective identity were in evident crisis. Born in Mexico City in 1962, she began to publish in the 1980s at a time of exceptionally varied and diverse poetic output by leading poets from several generations. In Mexico in the 1980s poetry was being written and published by Octavio Paz, Jaime Sabines, Gerardo Deniz, Tomás Segovia, José Emilio Pacheco, Gabriel Zaid, Jaime García Terrés, Ramón Xirau, Rubén Bonifaz Nuño, Marco Antonio Montes de Oca, Eduardo Lizalde, Homero Aridjis and Francisco Cervantes to mention only the more established poets of previous generations. But younger generations were also active and one of the unique characteristics of these more recent formations is the appearance and the abundance of female voices. For any poet starting to write at that time, the problem was the excessive number of models that were available. The poetic tradition in Mexico had always been strong, but the twentieth century represents something of a golden age in terms of the number, quality and diversity of lyrical voices.

In 1989 the Universidad Autónoma Metropolitana, a public university in Mexico City, published María's first book, *El jardín de los encantamientos* (*The Garden of Enchantments*). What immediately drew the attention of some readers was the ambition of this long poem, divided into a sequence of numbered parts with longer pieces alternating with shorter ones. Moving between dreams and memory, the poet recreated a world of amazement and abundance with a surprisingly rich and fluid vocabulary. Childhood was captured and transmitted in an atmosphere of legend, myth and magic. This was autobiographical poetry, identified by the choice of epigraph: verses from William Wordsworth, perhaps the greatest autobiographical poet of the English-language tradition. Some years earlier, in 1975, the greatest modern Mexican poet, Octavio Paz, had left an astounding example of the possibilities of autobiographical poetry in *Pasado en claro* (translated into English by Eliot Weinberger as *A Draft of Shadows*), a long poem that also took its epigraph from verses of *The Prelude*. It was certainly a hard act to follow and it must have seemed quite daunting for someone who was just starting. Most fledglings find it easier to find their way into poetry through shorter compositions and their first book is invariably a selection of brief poems written as part of their apprenticeship. Yet María chose to publish a long poem for her maiden voyage and she has continued to exploit this form in later works. In this first book, the reader is introduced to an extraordinarily receptive vision of the natural world and to a particular sensibility that is attentive to the pristine splendors of the marine landscape. For this incipient voice, poetry is something to be lived and re-lived as a journey through memory, dreams and the imagination: the poet recreates in all its playful vividness the sacred innocence of the first day.

The book offered here, together with the translation by Lorna Shaughnessy, is María's second outing, published originally in Mexico City by Ediciones del Equilibrista in 1990. Since this book she has seen eight more collections printed, the most recent being *Dylan y las ballenas* or *Dylan and the Whales* (2003). Her poetry has been translated into French by Fabienne Bradu and she has published in many of the best magazines and cultural supplements both in Mexico and abroad. Since the late 1980s examples of her work can be found in several of the most representative anthologies of new Mexican poetry, most recently in *Reversible Monuments: Contemporary Mexican Poetry*, by Mónica de la Torre and Michael Wiegers (Copper Canyon Press, 2002) and in the special number (23–24, Winter 2002–2003) of the excellent poetry review *Rosa Cúbica*, edited in Barcelona by Alfonso Alegre and Victoria Padilla, a number dedicated to modern Mexican verse. Since she began publishing, María has received many grants and prizes in recognition of her talent and dedication, including the Mexican National Prize for Poetry in 2003.

This, her second book of poetry, is dedicated to "Maqroll el Gaviero", the famous fictitious creation of the Columbian poet and novelist Álvaro Mutis who has lived in Mexico for most of his life, and it was due to the enthusiasm of Mutis that María's book was published. The enthusiasm is understandable as the world of this *Fábula* shares some of the features immortalized by Mutis. The narrative tone that allowed Mutis to transit invisibly from his powerful poetry to his more popular novels also appears in Baranda's poem, which shares with Mutis its nomadic qualities and reminiscences of Saint-John Perse.

This book represents another ambitious work: not a single long poem but a series of three 'readings', which are compositions closely linked by thematic and formal questions. Although its possibility was denied over a century ago by Edgar Allan Poe, the long poem has been one of the great achievements of modern Western verse. Outstanding examples exist in different traditions: from Whitman to Eliot, Pound, Crane, Williams, Bunting, Merrill and Ashbery; from Mallarmé to Valéry and Saint-John Perse; and, in Latin America, from Huidobro to Neruda and Zurita. In Mexico, the long poem has been a particularly fertile form for poets ever since Sor Juana Inés de la Cruz adopted it at the end of the seventeenth century for her most ambitious and personal composition, *Primer sueño*. In the twentieth century, the Mexican poet Gorostiza used it for his masterpiece in *Muerte sin fin* or *Endless Death* (1939) while many of the most important poems by Paz adopt this same form. It is the perfect vehicle for the personal and subjective epic of the modern age.

Although the conquest of Mexico was initially a male enterprise, carried out by conquistadors, evangelizers and colonists, the female component soon arrived from beyond the ocean and quickly became a repository of linguistic and cultural memory. As Baudelaire knew, dreams and the imagination are the best travel vehicles and nowhere makes a more fascinating destination than the origins of a culture. Any exploration of the origins of Mexican culture leads us inevitably to two great sources: the pre-Hispanic cosmogonies and the Spanish cultural legacy. Both exist in the poetry of María Baranda. She believes that Mexico is a place of voices, the voices that come from history, tradition and myth. The first voices heard in childhood are those of the mother and the other female figures that abound in any Mexican family. The poetic possibilities of maternal language, explored memorably by the Peruvian César Vallejo, are varied and inexhaustible. Through dreams and the imagination, María Baranda invents a kind of liquid communication between past and present in the form of the voices that speak in this *Fábula*. This is not dramatic poetry in the technical sense, but it does employ dramatic techniques and the reader can appreciate how in the first and longest of the three texts, "The Fishes' Tale", there is a deliberate attempt to contrast and alternate the different voices in counterpoint fashion and even differentiate them by typographical means.

Like all fables, this one is made of fiction, myth and invention. Like all fables, it is a linguistic construct. If there is communication between the past and the present, between the dead and the living, between the old world and the new world, what makes this communication possible is language itself as a living entity. Poetry has often been defined as the collective memory of a tribe, a nation or a culture. We know that without memory there is no identity. The poetry of María Baranda is an exploration of personal and collective identity using the medium of language not just to recuperate the past but also to 'create' memory in order to be able to live in the present. Towards the end of her first book we find a reference to women as the "engendradoras de la primera palabra"; if women engendered "the first word", one of the tasks of the poet is to reconstitute this language in all its strange inclusiveness.

Centro de Estudios Lingüísticos y Literarios
El Colegio de México

Olwen Rowe

Caveat Lector

María Baranda's *Fábula de los perdidos* moves deftly and seamlessly between an astonishing range of textual sources, including the Bible, *The Aeneid* and the Mayan *Popol Vuh*, the three main narrative threads which find new expression here. This poem bears testament to Baranda's remarkable ability to transform myth, history and ritual into dreamlike – and sometimes nightmarish – poetry. While the wealth of allusions lends the poems a timeless, universal quality, Baranda cleverly exploits the universality inherent in creation myths from various traditions. In this way, she captures the syncretism – the blending without loss of either tradition – of Western and indigenous cultures in the Americas. Many of the images bring together recognisable Judeo-Christian, Graeco-Roman and Mesoamerican traditions and beliefs.

I intend the annotations to be a rough and incomplete guide for the reader travelling into the magical world of Baranda's *Fábula*. They clarify some of the more obvious and important textual and cultural allusions in the poem. Indeed, much of the initial intellectual pleasure to be derived from reading *Fábula* is to be found in the process of unravelling the intertextual threads from which much of the text is woven. However, the annotations carry with them a *caveat lector*: the tidiness of annotations, with their inherent suggestion of metanarrative, or metanarratives, runs contrary to the spirit of the poem itself.

The wealth of allusions may lead us to conclude that it is possible to reconstruct a narrative from the fragments of the myths and histories to which the poem refers. This is not the case. The poem repeats, again and again, the impossibility of narrative coherence. A preoccupation with the loss of the ability to tell stories, and the essential role this plays in the construction of identity, is consistent throughout *Fábula*. In the poem, the permeating sense of loss finds its most pointed articulation in the recurring unfinished statement: "Si hemos perdido nuestras fábulas ...", "If we have lost our oldest tales ...". The loss of the ability to narrate implies the loss of the ability to communicate the identity of the tribe. Here, the stories have been lost, as well as the capacity to navigate them. The reader cannot escape this.

We are ultimately faced with a total lack of closure. The resounding "¿dónde?", "where?" of the lines which evoke the burning city of Troy becomes more insistent as we read. The question recalls the Medieval poetic device of *Ubi sunt?* (where are they now?). Twice the poem asks "¿Dónde la vida,/dónde?/Si hemos perdido nuestras fábulas ...", "Where are we to look for life?/Where?/If we have lost our oldest tales ...". Later these lines become "¿Dónde la vida,/dónde?/Si sólo quedan los perfumados cuerpos de las ahogadas ...", "Where are we to look for life?/Where?/If all that remains are the perfumed bodies of the drowned women ...". The great heroes of the epics are gone and the very stories which give meaning to reality have been lost. All that remains is the disturbing liminal image of "las ahogadas", "the drowned women".

Though the cultural source of the drowned women is clear – it derives from the belief that the Maya ritually drowned young sacrificial women in *cenotes*, sacred natural water wells – within the context of the poem the image of "las ahogadas" retains its disquieting ambiguity. While *Fábula* obliquely refers to many metanarratives, these bodies literally float up and disrupt the text with their unexplained presence, and the interrupted or truncated narratives which their presence seems to imply. In the context of recent Latin American and global disasters, these figures are also reminiscent of fleeing refugees or the bodies of the disappeared.

We become increasingly aware that both historical and mythical narratives of discovery are predicated on untold or untellable loss. *Fábula* insists that the dream of an idealistic syncretism of European and indigenous Mesoamerican cultures barely conceals a more sinister reality. During the early twentieth century the idealistic discourse of *mestizaje*, the racial and cultural intermixing of Spanish and indigenous Latin-

American was promoted in Mexico, presenting a new man, the *mestizo*, as the new Mexican. But the discourse of *mestizaje* often conceals an acculturation of the less dominant, indigenous culture and a less than utopian reality for the indigenous themselves. While this Mexican context rarely fades in *Fábula*, the poem is compelling because Baranda powerfully taps into the *zeitgeist* of the twentieth and twenty-first centuries, which Said dubbed 'the age of the refugee, the displaced person, mass migration'.[1] The poem may be read as an extended meditation on exile and dislocation.

Although *Fábula* is replete with the echoes of narratives that appear to guide the reader, ultimately we are set adrift in the poem. When we enter the enchanted world of *Fábula* we do so knowing that we are in danger of becoming the 'navegantes perdidos en las fábulas', 'voyagers lost in legend'. It is that experience of loss which may be most rewarding. The mastery of *Fábula* through annotations, for instance, is an illusory pleasure. As Barthes argues, the 'pleasure of the text is not necessarily a triumphant, heroic, muscular type'. He compels the reader to 'distinguish euphoria, fulfillment, comfort [...], from shock, disturbance, loss, which are proper to ecstasy, to bliss.'[2] Perhaps the best way to read *Fábula de los perdidos* is not to ask from where the images ensue, what they tell us, or what the poem means, but instead to experience the force behind the images of dislocation and to literally feel at a loss. Therein lies the more disquieting pleasure.

National University of Ireland, Galway

References

1 Edward W. Said, 'Reflections on Exile' in *Reflections on Exile and Other Essays* (Cambridge, MA: Harvard University Press, 2000), p. 174.

2 Roland Barthes, *The Pleasure of the Text*, trans. Richard Miller (New York: The Noonday Press 1989), pp.18–19.

Lorna Shaughnessy

TRANSLATOR'S NOTE

Every act of translation is approached with trepidation. And rightly so. The desired balance between respect for the original work, the culture and language it stems from, and the possible insights and transformations offered by the translator's language, culture and creativity seems, more often than not, unachievable. It is tempting to throw our hands in the air, cry "not possible" and give up. But today, in the face of relentless cultural and economic globalization, the practice of translation is more important than ever. It reminds us of the possibility of real intercultural dialogue, and that intercultural relations do not have to end in domination. The translation and dissemination of literature and other cultural products from non-anglophone cultures is of particular importance in this regard. More than any other linguistic culture, we tend only to listen to ourselves in the English speaking world, listen to only our versions of our histories, our myths, our tales, our *Fábulas*. We need to be reminded of the existence of other versions of our stories, and of the existence of other mythologies and histories. This is one of the reasons why I was attracted to María Baranda's *Fábula de los perdidos*.

In translating the title I was faced with what seemed an insurmountable example of difference. In Spanish usage, *fábula* is closely associated with the concept and process of weaving a narrative, telling a tale, whereas in English, the term fable is usually limited to the genre of parable or a moral tale, not at all appropriate to Baranda's poem. There is a distant etymological connection between the English 'fable' and the concept of fictionalisation, but it is not the dominant association with the word in common usage. This lack of an 'equivalent' for *fábula* undoubtedly represents a loss in the translation from the

Spanish to the English. In the title, and throughout the poem, I have opted for the term 'tale', a term broad enough to encompass many narrative genres, whether myth, legend or folktale. And given the poem's primary thematic concern with exploring issues of origin, whether geographic, cultural or linguistic, I opted for a line from the poem itself as title: "If we have lost our oldest tales" is a fear that haunts "The Fishes' Tale", the first section of the poem.

As already indicated in Anthony Stanton's Preface, and elucidated by Olwen Rowe's notes, *Fábula de los perdidos* contains a wealth of allusions to Classical European, Mesoamerican and Christian mythical narratives. This level of intertextuality does not, in and of itself, present a particular challenge to the translator. The challenge I encountered stemmed from Baranda's decision not to reveal the various identities of the tellers of the many tales that make up her poem. These narratives are recalled throughout the poem by a series of unidentified subjects, shifting from a third person italicised 'narrative voice' to a masculine singular first person 'I', and a feminine first person plural 'we'. In this way, *Fábula de los perdidos* certainly challenges what Lawrence Venuti has described as:

> the dominant poetics in Anglo-American culture, specifically its romantic assumptions; that the poet is a unified subjectivity freely expressing his personal experience, and that the poem should therefore be centred on the poet's self in transparent language.[1]

The identity of each voice is unnamed. The gender of each is only made known to the reader in the original text through the use of associated masculine or feminine adjectives. This is possible in Spanish because of its suppression of the personal pronoun in general, and its reliance on the conjugated verb to identify the speaker. What I have not been able to reproduce in the English is the degree of ambiguity around the identity of each voice that the Spanish creates. They cannot be pinned down by name or even pronoun.

In keeping with the author's wishes, I have endeavoured not to leave Spanish words untranslated in the text, with the exception of the Spanish term *mestiza,* whose ethnic connotations (the mixture of American indigenous and European) are so culturally specific I felt it better to preserve the original.

Finally, I hope to capture in this translation some of the lyricism of Baranda's poem, particularly the ebbs and flows of its tidal rhythms, to transmit some of the visual impact of her rich and varied imagery, and invite the non Spanish-speaking reader into the ancient and new worlds of tales that are transformed with every telling.

National University of Ireland, Galway

Reference

1 Venuti, Lawrence, *The Translator's Invisibility: A History of Translation,* (Routledge, London/NY 1995), p.279.

Fábula de los perdidos

If We Have Lost Our Oldest Tales

LECTURA PRIMERA

FIRST READING

Relato de los peces

Rompe la noche sus amarras,
abre el tiempo de su cautiverio,
y como una barca se agolpa
en el ondeo de las aguas.

Venimos de más allá de las arenas.
Hemos andado
por los senderos de la voz y el nombre
que los hombres guardan bajo sus párpados.

Navega por el lago de los pensamientos
donde fangosos gigantes ofician el rito
de quien duerme.

Cruzamos el mar cual gente extraña,
y en un puerto baldío
tendimos nuestro asombro al ver
«tres alcatraces, un garjao
y un rabo de junco».
Cónyuges fuimos del silbo de los pájaros,
del rumor que humeaba junto al polvo.
Sagradas doncellas en la ceremonia
de los náufragos,
siempre vestidas con piedras preciosas y escamas
en la víspera de la despedida.

Astros eternos,
dioses marinos
yacen inertes en el sueño de la superficie.
Su olor a grasa nos envuelve ...

The Fishes' Tale[1]

Night breaks free from its moorings,
raising the anchors of time,
and like a small boat lurching
strains against the swelling tide.

We came from beyond the sands,
walking the word paths,
the path whose name is hidden
behind the lids of closed eyes.

Cast adrift across the lake of thinking
where muddied giants celebrate
the rite of the sleeper.

We crossed the sea as strangers do,
and coming to an empty harbour
surrendered our disbelief when we saw
"three gannets, a river-bird like a pelican
and the streaming white tail of the tropicbird".[2]
We were wedded to their piping song
and the droning voices that rose with the dust.
Vestal virgins in the ceremony of the castaways,
ritually dressed in precious stones
and scales
on the eve of departure.

Ever-burning stars,
divine creatures of the deep
lie prostrate in the spent sleep of the shallows.
The smell of their decay overwhelms us …

Hemos visto al mar cubrir su piel
con plantas de la dársena
como un enorme ataúd de fuego a mediodía.
Pero de noche,
cuando las toninas saltan
para alcanzar a Dios
y el pez anuncia maravillas,
hemos visto a nuestros sueños
despojarse de sus plumas,
soltar su cabellera púrpura
y abrir sus huesos a las aguas niñas.
Y sobre la playa
donde el cangrejo,
voraz sacerdote,
le da muerte a un caracol
y los corales yacen ebrios en su fortuna,
oímos al silencio frágil desnudar
la voz hendida de la lluvia
en el revuelo de aquellas plumas
ofrecidas al sol,
que nos visita en la mañana
como un amante
                    volador,
y alza nuestros gemidos
sobre el montículo de los prodigios.
Él, un día en el mar y otro
en el blanco abismo de la ciudad,
«nos precipita a vernos cara a cara a los ojos»,
enrojecidas y tibias,
pero indefensas,
junto a los viejos astros, padres
de los relámpagos.

We have seen the sea cover its skin
with flowers from the dockside
like a blazing coffin in the midday sun.
But at night,
when the great tuna leap
high enough to touch their God
and the fish heralds miraculous events,
with our own eyes we have seen our dreams
shed their plumage,
untie their blue-black hair
and lay bare their bones to the young waters.
And on the beach,
where the crab,
like an insatiable priest,
sacrifices yet another victim
and the drunken coral wallows in its good fortune,
we listen to the brittle silence
undress the rain's rent voice
as our dream-feathers rise
in flurried tribute to the sun
who visits us each morning,
                              fleeting
as a secret lover,
and carries the sound of our moans
up to the top of the hill of portents.
One day in the sea, the next
in the glaring void of the city,
he is the one who
"hastens us to look into each others' eyes",[3]
hot, red-rimmed,
but defenceless
before the oldest stars, begetters
of lightening-bolts.

Alabados prófugos de Troya,
de los muros de ardientes soldados.
¿Dónde la luna, las ciudades antiguas
empedradas con profecías?
¿Dónde el Andrógino, la primera fortuna,
los enredados cabellos de Casandra?

Cruzamos el mar cual gente extraña.
Soñábamos, dormidas en el fondo de esos ojos,
toda la inmensidad
de los valles benditos por lenguas de vaca.
Todo el aliento de los santuarios
erguidos en la leyenda
de árboles misericordiosos.
Soñábamos,
con los párpados atados a la espuma
y el aire enhiesto y profético
de una ciudad marina.

¿Dónde la vida,
dónde?
Si hemos perdido nuestras fábulas ...

No fuimos aquellas que murieron
bajo el sermón de un pálido arcoiris,
desamparadas y sonámbulas,
en un mercado de retacerías.
No fuimos las mestizas
de rústicas mentiras, hechizadas
bajo la mano azul del brujo.
Tampoco las muñecas vestidas de lujuria
en dormitorios de marea.
Ni aquéllas melancólicas de lágrimas tatuadas
desde muy lejos,
que fueron enterradas con la memoria

Esteemed Trojans, fugitives
from the walls of burning infantry.[4]
Where is the moon now, where the ancient cities
paved with prophecy?
Where is Hermaphroditus, the first fate?
Where is Cassandra's uncombed hair?

We crossed the sea as strangers do.
We dreamed, sleeping in the depths of those eyes,
of the immeasurable vastness
of valleys blessed by the tongues of cows.
All the life of the shrines
that towered in the legend
of merciful trees.
We dreamed,
unable to tear our closed lids from the spray,
or the soaring, soothsaying wind
that blows through the city of the deep.

Where are we to look for life?
Where?
If we have lost our oldest tales …

We were not the women who died
beneath the homily of a faded rainbow,
homeless sleepwalkers
in the trinket-sellers' market.
Neither were we the *mestiza* daughters
of vulgar lies, spellbound
by the blue-handed wizard.[5]
Nor the sluttishly dressed dolls
in dockside bedrooms.
Nor those joyless women from distant shores
with tears tattooed on their cheeks,
now buried in a plot with memory

y la nostalgia.
Nunca estuvimos en los muelles maléficos
del marino perdido.
Ni en los vitrales tristes y milagrosos
de húmedas catedrales.
¡Ah!, pero en la noche,
cuando se fraguan risas en soledad
y reverberan las olvidadas imágenes
de una mar que se abre y ruge,
en aquel oleaje de misterio
que urde a la tierra fabulosa con sus gritos,
allí estuvimos,
frescas
en la agonía del tiempo,
mortales
como un pequeño gato soberbio y femenino,
vírgenes
de grandes familias,
locas
que se levantan a medianoche
para amaestrar desnudas
a un ardiente camastro de víboras,
y luego,
cariñosas,
ofrecerles el agua blanca de sus pechos.
Nuestro sueño era el sueño de los marinos.

Rompe la noche sus amarras,
navega.
Atrás quedó un palacio
de patios desérticos y de atrios
donde la joven loca está cercada por sus hijas.

and nostalgia.
We never strayed into the hellish docks
of the lost sailor,
never saw the sad miracle of stained-glass
in damp Cathedrals.
But at night, at night,
when laughter is forged from solitude
and all the forgotten images
of a sea that opens its jaws and roars
resonate in the mysterious rhythm of a heavy swell
that conjures a fabled land with its clamour,
we were there in the night,
fresh
to the agonies of time,
frail
and proud as a she-cat,
virgins
from large families,
madwomen
who rise naked at midnight
to tame
a burning bedful of vipers,
and then,
tenderly,
offer them the white water of their breasts.
Our dream was the dream of mariners.

Night breaks loose from its moorings
and sets sail.
Left behind is a palace
with empty courtyards and columns,
where the mad girl's daughters surround her.[6]

Soñábamos, y a lo lejos oímos
una lengua muerta que nos decía:
No soy sino la sombra húmeda
e infinita
donde el viento hunde su discurso.
Encerrado en mi labor de ciego
vivo como una enfermedad del trópico
que agoniza lenta a la orilla
del sepulcro.
¡Mírenme! Estoy con las gaviotas,
golpeando cordilleras de miseria
y de apariciones.
Vivo con el bullicio y la gritería
de una ciudad vecina,
cerca de un altar de alumbre
y de pequeñas mutilaciones.
Yo sostuve el Arca de la Alianza.
Sobre mí tendieron el manto de oro
del listado eterno,
pintado del color de las orquídeas.
Fui el eco jadeante
del amante ajeno,
el suplicio que los apartaba
de los vivos,
la vida redonda e ingrávida
en el espejo de sus adivinanzas.
El que siempre aguardaba
como una piedra negra
en los lugares muertos.
El que pintan de jade y plata
en los jarrones y las vajillas
de porcelana.
Las mujeres cuando vienen aquí
traen sombreros inmensos
a los ojos del pájaro.

We dreamed, and from a distance
heard a dead tongue speak to us:
I am no more and no less
than the infinite, damp abyss
where the wind hurls its sermons.
Shut away in my blindman's work
like a tropical disease,
slowly dying on
sepulchred shores.
Look, here I am, home of the gulls,
beating against dispossessed mountains,
the sites of apparitions.
And here again in the rush and clamour
of a neighbouring port,
beside an altar of smoking stones
covered in mementos of a thousand wounds.[7]
I am the one who bore the Ark of the Covenant.
The golden robe of the chosen few
was placed on my shoulders,
painted the colour of orchids.
I was the panting echo
of another's lover,
the sentence passed down that set you
apart from the living,
the weightless orb of life
in your divining mirror.
I am the one who has always waited,
as certain as black stone
in dead places.
The one they paint in jade and silver
on urns and vessels
of the finest porcelain.
From above, where the birds fly,
the women who come here
seem to wear immense hats.

Y los niños,
que saben más de mí
bajo los párpados,
alzan castillos de sal,
copas de polvo y paraíso
donde el náufrago bebe la soledad.
¡Mírenme! Voy en las pupilas
de aquella adolescente adolorida,
en la risa de la vieja vendedora de pescado
que nos ofrece
el ritual secreto de sus labios,
voy en la falda de aquella campesina gorda y ronca,
solitaria reina de los campos.
Y en una mesa de mantel de lluvia
soy el eterno alarido del ahogado.

¡Ah! cautiva agorera
que sube al lecho de los victoriosos
y sabe de astros y de aves,
del anuncio celeste que resplandece
en el brebaje de la arena.
Ella, la esposa con ojos de niño
se pasea lenta y sola
por un bosque de columnas erguidas
en los sueños.
Mujer abierta a la noche entera, su cuerpo
brama espumoso al mar, y él,
ardiente y ansioso,
se levanta con hondo gemido
para alcanzar su destino fatal.
¿Dónde la vida,
dónde?
Si hemos perdido nuestras fábulas ...

And the children,
who know more of me
beneath their closed eyelids,
build castles out of salt,
cups filled with paradise and ashes
where the castaway drinks his solitude.
Look at me! In the pained eyes
of that young girl,
in the old fishwife's laugh,
taunting us
with the secret she keeps behind her curling lip,
or hidden behind the ample skirts
of the woman who works the land,
plump and hoarse,
the solitary queen of the cornfields.
And at the table covered in a cloth of rain,
I am the ever-present wailing of the drowned.

Ah, clairvoyant slave
who climbed into the victors' bed
and understands the ways of the stars and the birds,
who sees the heavens' signs
shine forth from the caked sand.
Wife with a child's eyes
who slowly walks alone
through a forest of tall columns
erected in dreams.
A woman who calls out to the sea, her body
open to the endless night, seething in anticipation,
while the sea, all hot craving,
rises up with a deep moan
to meet its final destiny.
Where are we to look for life?
Where?
If we have lost our oldest tales …

Mas allí, sobre las aguas,
cual luminoso espejismo,
vimos una ciudad esculpida en el vacío,
donde la sonrisa de un sol invisible
deja atónitas nuestras miradas.

Los náufragos visitan cumbres
y llanuras líquidas al alba,
bajo un cielo airoso que hace la delicia de quien lo mira.
Los sin nombre.
Los de carne de sal que guardan su infancia
con los pájaros
abren un lamento de luz hacia las aguas:
«¡Ah, olas ... más olas ... y el cansancio abruma ...
y tanto mar que por cruzar nos falta ...!»
Aquella tierra se cubrió con nubes,
y de las nubes surgió un grupo de matronas
que arrullaron las canciones tristes e insípidas
con la caridad de yerbas santas.

Fuimos envueltas de súbito
con el hinojo, el enebro
y el meliloto;
con llanos y montes
y un aguacero espléndido
de fábulas.

Bellas,
cual delfines en Los Cárpatos
o rosas negras
en manos de un prófugo del Asia,
dormían,
cuando a la mar
nos fuimos en el Arca.

But there, above the waters
like a shimmering mirage,
we saw a city sculpted in the empty air,
and our astonished eyes met
a smiling, invisible sun.[8]

The castaways reach the highest peaks
and cross liquid plains to meet the dawn
beneath a gracefully arching sky, delightful
to the eyes of all who behold it.
The nameless ones.
The ones with salt in their blood
who put aside their childhood like songbirds,
cast a dawn lament out on the waters:
"How many more waves to make us weary,
how wide a sea must we still cross?"[9]
And from the clouds that cloaked the land
came a band of pious women
crooning their sad, tired songs
with the cold comfort of medicinal herbs.

Suddenly we were halted by
the perfume of fennel, juniper
and sweet yellow clover,
between mountains and plains,
drenched by a dazzling cloudburst
of legends.

Beautiful
as dolphins in the Carpathians,
or black roses
in the hands of a fugitive from Asia,
they slept
as we sailed forth
in the Ark.

«*Los aires eran muy dulces y sabrosos.*»
«*A Dios muchas gracias sean dadas*»
porque del otro lado,
como una ceremonia
entre las redes perdidas de los marineros,
fueron llevadas
a gritos
en el aflujo de la noche,
en la vertiente de imágenes purificadas
rugiendo en su dolor,
entre piedras que hacían muros fríos
y secretos
en la plenitud de su estremecimiento;
fueron arrastradas
a las tierras nuevas, ruidosas
por el amor de los líquenes con los helechos.
Tierras de verdes mediodías redondos
bajo un sol de hace tanto tiempo.
Nidos de pájaros solitarios poblaban
los pliegues desconocidos de aquel país
de telas de arcilla y de arena.
Largos cabellos ondulados hacían las playas,
donde pálidas lámparas recibían
los perfumados cuerpos de las ahogadas.

¡Ah!, te elegimos a ti en el colmo
de la tristeza.
Cuando nuestros rostros, frescos
como el aceite de una nuez inmutable
en su esencia,
se tiñeron de una leche nueva,
y la púrpura cáscara del higo
pintó los restos de esa noche
en nuestros cuerpos.

"The winds were light and perfumed".
"Give thanks to Almighty God",[10]
and from the farthest shore
they were dragged
ceremoniously
from sailors' lost nets,
screaming
in the all-engulfing darkness,
in the outpouring of purged images,
crying out in horror
to the stones that would build cold,
secret walls
at the very apex of their pain;
they were dragged
to new lands, made mad
for the love of lichens and ferns.
A world of fulsome green days
lit by a sun as old as time.
Like a clay-coloured cloth the land
folded, and in its hidden creases
solitary birds built their nests.
Its beaches were long tresses of curling hair
where pale lamps brought ashore
the perfumed bodies of drowned women.[11]

Ah yes, it was you we chose from the depths
of sorrow.
When our faces, fresh
as the enduring essence of the
walnut's oil,
were stained a new colour,
and the remains of that night
were branded on our bodies
with the purple of fig-skin.

¡Ah!, te elegimos a la entrada de los puertos
donde las mujeres más jóvenes
sueñan
con los viajes de los patos silvestres
a la Antártida.
Te elegimos a la salida de las aguas,
al comienzo de las historias y las leyendas
ávidas de olas más altas.
Te elegimos por encima de las velas
que atraviesan el amplio reino de los vientos,
mientras el grito de la garza
se abre como herida que embellece a la marea.
«Tú fuiste el elegido,
contigo estableceré mi pacto.»

¿Dónde la vida,
dónde?
Si sólo quedan los perfumados cuerpos de las ahogadas ...

Pensábamos, hurgando la sal de toda alga,
la sangre submarina de los náufragos,
en los afeites y los aromas que estremecen
a los cuerpos bajo sus ropas;
en los sabores de las plazas públicas
envanecidas por el color de la fruta
y el uso de toda pedrería.
Pensábamos
en el remanso de una ruina de palabras
asentada bajo la historia de las alturas.
Fatigadas ante los márgenes de la tierra
conocimos todo camino
que conducía a los sanatorios.

Yes, we chose you at the point of entry to harbours
where the youngest of women
dream
of the wild ducks' journeys
to the Antarctic.
We chose you at the river-mouth,
the launching-place of legends and tales
that seek higher waves.
We chose you above all the sails
that cross the wide kingdom of the winds,
while the heron's cry
opens like a wound,
a final flourish on the water.
"Yes, you are the chosen one,
with you I will make my covenant."[12]

Where are we to look for life?
Where?
If all that remains are the perfumed bodies of the drowned ...

We thought, brushing salt from scraps of seaweed,
underwater blood from the bodies of the shipwrecked,
about the lotions and perfumes that thrill
the body beneath its clothes;
about the many flavours of town squares
grown vain with the colour of fruit stalls
and the flaunting of precious jewels.
We thought
about the pool of ruined words that lies
at the foot of the tale of tall mountains.
Exhausted at the sight of the ends of the earth
we travelled every path
that led to a madhouse.

Allí, sobre largos tablones de madera,
sangramos nuestro origen en la memoria
de las hijas. Madres fuimos
de la escoria que maravilla
a las aves agoreras y a las águilas
cuando descienden,
de ciudad en ciudad,
buscando el hambre y la miseria.
El mar lamía nuestros vientres de piedra.
Había signos de aquel matrimonio
con las aguas,
en la arborescencia de los corales
y en los movimientos de la noche
sobre las playas.
Envejecíamos,
y nuestros cuerpos,
libres de toda claridad,
se embalsamaban con el rastrojo de las dragas.

Navega la noche por la mar de fondo.
«Amarga espuma en torno a él sus monstruos
en festivas cabriolas levantaba.»
El tiempo oscuro. La tempestad en calma
y el sol,
en su lejano albergue,
lamía la frente de la caliza y la obsidiana.

Moríamos a ras de mar.
bajo el suplicio de los rabihorcados
y la cárdena acogida de emperadores
y peces dorados
diciendo el Salve Regina
que los marineros recitaban
sobre sus lechos de agua.

There, on long wooden benches,
our birthright bled away in our
daughters' memories. We were mothers
to the human dross that gapes, awe-struck,
at birds of ill-omen and eagles
as they descend
from city to city
in search of human misery and hunger.
The sea lapped at our wombs of stone.
There were premonitions of that coupling
with the seas,
in the ever-branching corals
and the way the night moved
across the beaches.
We grew old,
and our bodies,
released from all clarity,
were embalmed with mud dredged from the depths.

Night sails on the deepest of seas
"A mighty swell cavorted in monstrous forms,
sending far and wide its bitter spray."[13]
Time darkens. The storm retreats,
and the sun,
from its distant refuge,
licks the earth's brow of limestone and obsidian.[14]

We died at sea-level,
to the heart-rending cry of the black frigatebird,
the crimson torment of swordfish
and fish with golden scales,
mouthing the same Salve Regina[15]
the sailors recited
on their watery beds.

Moríamos,
y la luna emergía lenta
de entre las palmas.
Ascendía para reinar aquellos cuerpos
color de aceituna y de nopal.
Ninfa ella misma,
ardía en bajamar,
donde los remeros clavaban su ofrenda
hasta el fondo de los amoríos.

La mar cantaba a solas
aquel dulce rumor en sus honduras.
El viento narraba las hazañas
de más allá de las arenas.
De la tierra brotaban árboles,
y de los árboles,
la sangre verde de las batallas.

Nosotras,
tan lejos aún de las alturas,
enloquecíamos
con el bramido de las olas.
Viajeras sin fin de la memoria,
escuchamos las blasfemias de las algas
y el tedio de la perca en la caleta.
Y no había más consuelo
que la constelación mal amada
del silencio:

Hosanna, hosanna,
bendito es el señor de nuestro sueño.

Mendigas de la sal y de la espuma
buscaron la pureza sobre las aguas y las tierras;
en el aroma de las hojas y la frescura de las yerbas;

We died,
and the moon slowly emerged
from behind the palm trees,
rising up to reign over those bodies,
as green as olive and nopal.[16]
Like a nymph,
radiant in the low tide,
where oarsmen sank their offerings
as deep as love itself.

In the lone voice of the sea
a murmuring song rose from the depths.
The wind told tales of great deeds
from beyond the sands.
Trees sprang from the earth,
and from the trees,
the green blood of battles.

And we women,
still so far from the mountains,
going steadily mad
with the pounding of the waves.
Voyagers with no end to our memory,
listening to the seaweed's blasphemies,
the perch's weary round in the small cove.
Our only consolation
the abandoned constellation
of silence.

Hosanna, hosanna,
blessed be the Lord of our dreams.

Beggar-women from the regions of salt and spray
looked for something pure over water and land;
in the smell of dry leaves and cool grasses;

sobre los esqueletos de las gaviotas
y el manto violáceo de la morera;
en los santuarios y los rituales
de las vírgenes del agua;
en el ritmo de los aretes y las ajorcas
y en las laminillas que cuelgan de las pulseras;
en el olor de la azalea y la violeta
y en la manera rápida y prodigiosa de bordar el amor
sobre las sábanas;
en la mirada sonámbula de las videntes
y el roce secreto de las viejas curanderas.
Ellas,
que defendieron los terraplenes y sedecías,
se apoderaron de plateas y aspersorios,
incensarios y calderas,
y de todo aquello que hacía el reino de los tiempos.

Era el tiempo de Orión
y eran nuestros hombres:
los reyes de los campos y príncipes
de las vacadas;
valientes caballeros tigre
y caballeros águila;
señores del poder y la batalla;
gobernadores de pueblos
y naciones de insectos;
observadores fantasmas que hacen honores
a la gente extraña;
navegantes de olas encrespadas
que encomendaron su vida a la esperanza;
los que al partir del puerto
no escuchan el adiós que los reclama;
los que portan un nombre victorioso;
hombres hambrientos del barro, la vasija
y el simulacro.

above the skeletons of gulls
and the purple mantles of mulberry trees,
in shrines and sacred rites
to the virgins of the sea;
in the jangling rhythm of earrings,
of bangles and charms dangling from wrists;
in the smell of violets and azaleas
and the legendary quickness of the hand that embroiders love
on its sheets;
in the dream-filled eyes of prophetesses
and the old healer-womens' secret touch.
Women
who held the ramparts and sacred places,
commanding trenches, aspersoria,
censers, ceremonial urns,
each and every thing devised under the reign of time.

It was the age of Orion[17]
and they were our men:
kings of pastures and princes of herds;
valiant knights of the order of the jaguar
and knights of the order of the eagle;[18]
powerful lords of battlefields,
governors over entire peoples
and insect nations;[19]
ghostly astronomers who paid homage
to strangers;
navigators of angry waves
who offered up their lives to hope;
men who never hear the goodbyes that claim them
as they sail out from harbours;
men who wear the name of victory;
hungry men made of clay,[20] both vessel
and mold.

Ellos,
en sus carros de sombra,
en sus ritos de sangre,
en el hondo abismo sin memoria.
Ellos: nuestros hombres.
Eligieron a «los nenúfares, los nelumbios,
la Victoria regia y los botones de oro».
¡Navegantes perdidos en las fábulas!
Supieron de las rojas terrazas de caliza
para los siervos del pensamiento;
de los pisos de cedro y de encino
para las bibliotecas,
y de largas galerías
en la misericordia de los preceptos.

Luces,
brillo de las diademas destazadas.
Estallidos que dejan intacto
aquel reposo de las aguas.

Con la música de las entrañas,
con las bocas obscenas que desde lejos
descifran los signos celestes
y el cándido balanceo de las palmeras,
cantamos a la muerte: nuestra pequeña reina.
Frente a la gente de la península
y los peces de la caleta,
frente a la tumba de una ciudad,
cantamos las formas de los deseos
atentas a las crónicas del sueño,
al soplo de las sibilas
y al esplendor de los espejos;
a las leyes de las riberas
y a los presagios del tiempo;

Men
with their shadowy chariots,
with their blood-rites,
in the deepest unremembering abyss.
Our men.
They chose water-lilies, lotus-flowers,
night-blooming Victoria lilies and crowfoot.
Voyagers lost in legend!
They learned about the limestone balconies
painted red for the slaves of reason;
the floors of cedar and holm-oak
laid in libraries;
and long passageways
in the compassion of commandments.

Lights,
the glitter of shattered diadems.
Explosions that leave unmoved
the resting waters.

With a music that comes from inside;
with foul tongues that read
heavenly portents from afar,
with the lulling rhythm of swaying palm trees,
we sang of death: our lesser queen.
Watched by the people of the peninsula
and the fishes in their little coves,
standing before a city's grave,
we sang of the many shapes of our desire,
listening for dreams foretold,
the sibyls' voice,
the mirrors' splendour;
for the laws of the tides
and presentiments of time;

a la brisa de la trompeta
y a la zarza ardiente de la guerra.
Cantamos,
con las manos vacías y la lengua extranjera,
en las bancas, en las calles, en las alcobas,
en el perfume de las adelfas,
el puro canto del poema.

A lo alto de los arrecifes
fue llevada la voz
como una crónica celeste.

Marinero,
canta una canción entre las rocas,
en los lugares del tiempo y la promesa
de volver a oír la voz
de la sirena.
Marinero del inútil regreso
hacia los puertos,
de la historia que los faros alumbran
en los valles muertos,
del silbo, a grandes gritos, de esos muertos
y de los días que apacientan
el lento avance del pelícano.
Marinero de la noche
que lamenta el ver morir a una gaviota.
Marinero sin más alma que las olas
y su diaria embestida cadenciosa.
Te desplazas,
respirando
el aroma de las aguas,
de los cabos, de las islas,
de los hijos perdidos y de la mujer
resplandeciente en la distancia.

for the breeze of bugle-call
and the burning scrub of war.
We sang
with empty hands and a strangers' tongue,
on benches, street-corners, and in bedrooms,
in the scent of oleander,
the pure song of poetry.

Like a celestial chronicle,
their voice was carried up
and up to the top of the reefs.

Sailor,
sing a song from the rocky
coasts of time, the promise
that once again we will hear
the siren's voice.[21]
Sailor who returned in vain
to home ports,
whose story flashes in a lighthouse beam
in dead valleys
that echo with the shrill cries of the departed
and long days that feed
the pelican's unhurried gait.
Sailor of the night
who grieves to see a seagull die.
Sailor with no soul but the daily,
rhythmic pounding of the waves.
Always moving,
inhaling
the salty aroma of oceans,
headlands, islands,
of children lost and the woman
who waits, resplendent, in the distance.

Marinero:
tu canto es el camino errante de los vientos.

Y hubo vientos al rayar el alba,
y los niños, vestidos de júbilo,
alabaron los áridos pasillos del desierto
donde un abuelo ciego
predicaba sus destinos:

De todas partes,
de las tierras lejanas e inmensas,
de los lugares perdidos en una lengua bárbara,
de los límites y reinos,
de los parajes floridos,
de los maizales, los nopaleros,
los dorados campos de Huexotzinco,
de los montes color de zapote,
de las regiones misteriosas de las flores,
de los magueyes,
del interior de las aguas
donde se escucha el grito del águila,
surgirán los niños,
enardecidos
por la arrogancia del mar.

«Sólo venimos a dormir,
sólo venimos a soñar:
¡No es verdad; no es verdad
que venimos a vivir en esta tierra!»

Caminaban solitarios, desnudos, silenciosos
por los nervios de la ciudad. Llevaban
una ofrenda de guirnaldas
y flores doradas. Seguían
el ruido de la mar. Iban,

Sailor:
your song is the errant path of the winds.

And the first ray of dawn brought wind,
and the children, decked out in their delight
sang the praises of dry desert tracks
where a blind old man
foretold their destinies:

From every corner of the earth,
from the most distant and vast lands,
from lost places and in barbarous tongues,
from borderlands and kingdoms,
from flowering fields,
cornfields and the homelands of the nopal,
the golden meadows of Huexotzinco[22]
and mountains black as sapote fruit,
from mysterious regions of flowers
and maguey agaves,
and from that place where the eagle's cry
resounds within the waters,
children will rise up,
inflamed
by the sea's arrogance.

"We come only to sleep
we come only to dream:
It is not true, not true
that we come to live in this land!"[23]

Alone, naked and in silence, they came
through the very nerves of the city, carrying
a garland offering
of golden flowers. They followed
the sound of the sea, walking

con los pasos del pastor, narrando
las obras del trueno
y el remolino de los vientos. Eran
un ejército de estrellas
al fondo de los cielos.
¡Gloria, gloria a las migraciones
de los niños que aguardan
la voz del altísimo!
Y con la risa y la exaltación de las aguas
bendijeron los bosques, las plazas
y las piedras más elevadas del abismo.

Pulsa el viento al cielo dócil.
Azota profecías.

Batallas bajo el sol.
Arden los niños.
Olvídense de sí - recita el viento -,
canten la vida mientras mueren.

Empujados por la sangre del exilio,
por lentas sílabas que brillan en su pelo,
trazan el horizonte,
sueñan el firmamento.
Su sueño son las aguas del marino.

with a shepherd's footstep, telling
tales of the thunder's deeds
and of great swirling winds. They were
an army of stars
in the depths of the skies.
Glory, glory be to the migrant
children who await
the voice from on high!
And to the sound of laughter and rapturous seas
they blessed the forests, the town square
and the highest rocks in the abyss.

The wind prods an impassive sky,
whipping up prophecies.

The sun beats down on battlefields.
Children burn.
Forget yourselves – commands the wind –
sing of life as you face death.

Spurred on by the blood of exile,
by the slow syllables still shining in their hair,
they trace a horizon,
dream up a firmament.
Their dream, the waters of the sea.

LECTURA SEGUNDA

SECOND READING

Epístola del náufrago

Tiempo hubo para la audiencia de los peces,
y los Escribas de la ley y la doctrina,
en la cadencia oculta de la noche calma,
dieron el nombramiento a los dioses de las aguas
buscando la alianza de los carámbanos,
la suave acometida de los rezos.

Y tiempo hubo también
en que todos los seres
de ciudades y villas,
de los largos tramos de tierra fresca,
hechizaron la lumbre, el agua
y el cálido linaje de los vientos.

Allí, los hombres de barro
pintaron el estremecimiento de los suelos,
    los atrios del desierto,
    los pórticos del alba,
    la calle de los perros.

Levantaron los muros de antiguas montañas
con la lejanía tatuada sobre el pecho,
como una voz sin dueño ni leyenda
o como el silencio que llevan los hombres de lejos.

Allí, gritaron las flores, las casas
que sólo aman el rojo filo de esa noche.
Y para ellas, los hombres del tiempo,
escucharon el anuncio de los pájaros del norte,
el bello canto de sus muertos:

The Castaway's Epistle

There was still time for the court of fishes,
and the Scribes of doctrine and law
spelt out the names of the sea-gods
in the dark pulse of a still night,
seeking the allegiance of icicles,
the gentle pledge of prayer.

And there was a time too
when all living creatures
from cities, towns,
long tracts of unspoiled land,
cast a spell on fire, water
and the winds' ardent lineage.

There it was, that men of clay
painted the shuddering earth,
    the inner courtyards of the desert,
    portals to the dawn,
    a street of dogs.

They raised walls of ancient mountains
with a distant shore tattooed on their chests,
like a voice with no tale or teller,
or the silence borne by men from afar.

There it was, that flowers cried out, roses
that love only the night's sharp red edge.
And for their sake alone, time-bound men
heeded omens of birds that would come from the north
in the sonorous chanting of their dead:

La tierra dormitaba
del otro lado de este mundo.
Bajo la ensoñación del cielo, amplia
era la superficie de la tierra,
con su cetro de sombra y de blancura
y sus lugares de piedra y arena.
La tierra hecha presente
tomaba forma humana
con el sabor de la demencia:

Yo soy el hijo, el padre, la madre,
el sufrimiento y la fuerza.
Soy el rugir del faro
y de la fábrica, el lento
acontecer del tiempo.
Soy el aroma del mar sereno,
la tempestad,
la fiesta de los viejos.
Sobre mí, fundo los días
del abejorro y de la abeja,
las bodas del hombre y de la bestia,
la idea de los demonios de ojos vivos
que danzan y conversan ligeros
y nos legan tan sólo el eco.

La tierra, en voz más baja,
arrullaba las yerbas de su piel.
La tierra vieja. La tierra fresca.
Era inútil cerrar los ojos,
dejar el testimonio en las plazas:

«De mar a mar entre los dos la guerra.»
El grito del marino,

The land slumbered
on the other side of the world.
Below a dreaming sky
the earth's surface spread wide
with its stony and sandy places,
its supreme play of light and shade.
And the earth took human form
tinged with madness,
and dwelt amongst us:

I am the son, the father, the mother,
suffering and strength.
I am the blaring fog-horn,
time's slow unfolding.
I am the scent of a calm sea,
thunder and lightening,
the celebrations of old men.
On this body I lay down the days
of the bees and wasps,
the couplings of man and of beast,
the first inkling of demons with shining eyes
whose nimble feet and tongues
leave us nothing but a hollow echo.

The land cooed in a hushed voice
to the sweet herbs that flourished on its skin.
Old land. New land.
No sleep behind closed eyes,
nor a life recounted in town squares:

"From sea to sea, between the two only war."[24]
The sailor's cry,

el cuerpo de la espada.
Y allá,
rebelde, incauta,
la hija, la hermana,
la sola ausencia de la mar:
la tierra en voz más baja.

Nosotros, tendidos ante los sueños de la Reina,
supimos la ley de los ciclones,
la estación de las fábulas,
la ronda de aquellos cielos de gaviotas.
Con el oficio de los Embajadores,
hablamos del homenaje de ríos y lagunas,
de convenciones, de extrañas cortezas,
de rutas de enebro y engarzadas palmeras.
Hablamos de la genealogía de los Templos,
de la piel de tejón, del paño de jacinto,
de la ceremonia en el límite de la impureza.
Nosotros, pájaros del norte, encadenamos
los lazos del Cielo y de la Tierra.

(Di la verdad hacedor de mentiras – reclama la Reina
con su boca de buenas familias.)

Pero la noche ha penetrado esa parte de la memoria
y las mujeres elevan sus rezos
en el hastío de tanta ofrenda.

 ¡Loadas aquellas tardes calmas
 en que las naves,
 cual cabras ciegas, regresaban
 a la memoria de su patria!

the breadth of the blade.
And there,
reckless and defiant,
daughter, sister,
the sea's solitary absence:
the land whispering ever-softer.

And we, prostrate before the dreams of a Queen,
learned the rules that govern cyclones,
the circling of skies alive with gulls,
and seasons of legend and fable.
With our titles of Ambassadors,
we paid homage to rivers and lakes,
spoke of councils and trees with strange bark,
juniper-routes and necklaces of palm trees.
We spoke of the Temples and their genealogy,
of badger-skin and sacred hyacinth cloth,[25]
the rite that marks the limits of impurity.
We were the birds from the north, fastening
chains between Heaven and Earth.

("Speak the truth, you fabricator of lies", demands the
Queen with her well-bred mouth.)

But dark night has penetrated that portion of memory,
and women send up their prayers
in the tedium born of too many offerings.

Blessed were the calm evenings
when ships' prows came nodding back
to the memory of a homeland, rising and falling
in the swell like the heads of blind goats!

¡Loada la familia de la cerasta,
el rey de los rebaños,
las historias contadas cara a cara!

¡Loadas las bahías abiertas
a los juegos de la luna,
a las correrías de noches asesinas!

¡Loado el hacedor de muelles
y alacenas
donde se guarda la gracia y la maravilla!

(Ah, respiramos el placer del orégano
y del canelo. Estamos listas para morir
sin remordimientos.)

¡Bendita la noche que alberga tanto sueño!

Y por encima de la dicha y de la gloria,
te rogamos Señor
nos concedas saber el curso de los vientos,
la ruta del primer crujido
y las leyes que erigen a los lirios.
Abriremos Señor
nuestro cuerpo
a las sierras, a los cañaverales
y a todo monte polvoriento.
Seremos dóciles
a los sudores de la selva,
dulces
a las voces de la piedra,
fieles
al tubérculo y a las costas

Blessed the horned viper's lineage,
king of the flocks
and stories told face to face!

Blessed the bays, wide open
to the moon's silver teasing,
the raids of murderous nights!

Blessed the builder of harbours
and stores
where laughter and wonder are stacked high!

(Ah, let us breathe in the pleasures of cinnamon
and oregano. We are ready to die
without remorse.)

Blessed is the night that houses so many dreams!

But more than any blessing
we pray, Oh Lord,
that you show us the way the winds blow,
which route to follow at the first creaking of the mast,
the powers that make the lily stand so tall.
And we shall open, Oh Lord,
our bodies
to the highest peaks, sugar-cane fields
and every dusty mountain that we meet.
We shall submit meekly
to jungle fevers,
answer sweetly
to the voices in the rocks,
be loyal subjects
to tubercular coasts

donde se comercia con la malaria
y la griseta.

Y por los labios de una dulce adivina
se desliza esta parte del sueño:
bajo el sabor de las yerbas amargas
y el espolón del viento,
va el hombre a la tierra antigua,
enviado a las cimas
y a los campos de labranza
para dejar huella en los libros.
El Adelantado
que nombra las cosas secretas, los abismales
y las figuraciones de la piedra, mastica
una hoja cultivada bajo la luna
y su pensamiento
desciende a las raíces de aquel imperio.

Cargado de historia
voy al principio de toda mirada.
Y con el don del altísimo,
privilegio ramas y montañas.

Echados los bateles a la mar
buscaba la bienaventuranza.
A más de seis leguas nacía la playa de sus anhelos.

Hete ahí, vasta en hojas de palma.
Harta en clases de peces,
ornada con la risa de sábalos y jureles.
Eres el cuerpo de una virgen

trading in malaria
and tree-rot.

And from the lips of a benevolent seer
slips this part of the dream:
with the taste of bitter herbs
and the ramming of the wind,
a man journeys to the old land,
dispatched to mountaintops
and tilled fields
so that proof could be written in books.
The Scout
gives names to unknown, unknowable things,
imaginings in stone; he chews
on a leaf sown by moonlight,
his thoughts
descending to the roots of that other empire.

    Weighed down by history,
    I must trace the source of every gaze.
    And by the grace of God
    bestow favours on mountains and boughs.

And putting out to sea,
he went in search of good fortune.
Six leagues out, he sighted the shoreline of his desires.

    And there you were,
    a never-ending rim of palm leaves
    with your countless species of fish,
    set off by the smiling shad and saurel.
    You, in your virgin's body

la túnica de la esperanza.
Sobre ti señalaré el honor y la casta.

¡Ah, Tierra de boca de mujer,
desata toda mi fuerza,
la gracia como fruto que anida
en la palmera de mi cuerpo!
Estoy solo y tengo miedo.
Lejana está la otra ribera de mi sueño,
el puerto donde mujeres de sal
pintan la faz de los deseos.
¡Huéspedes de mi dulce memoria,
coman de mí,
de mis recuerdos,
quiero oírlas roer el pan y el queso,
ser convidado como un buen remedo
para los muertos!
Palpita la tierra adentro de mis venas.
Siento la caliza, el fósforo,
la tregua de la raíz sin fondo.
Y la saliva de la tierra me encuentra
— hombre solo —
como a la hoja del lentisco
en el silbo que viene del mar.

Verde era la hoja que recordaban los viajeros.
Sentados sobre el viejo barandal de madera,
celebraban los caminos donde el cenzontle
anunciaba la vida.

Entregado al placer de los bledos
y de las jarcias,
veo las cosas inmóviles y absurdas
pensando en las mujeres que se ríen a solas.

and your tunic woven with hope.
On you I will bestow honour,
your issue will be the new ascendancy.

Land with a woman's mouth,
unbind my strength,
the charms that nestle like fruit
in the tall palm of my body!
I am alone and afraid.
The other shore of my dreams is distant now,
the port where women with salt on their skin
paint a face for every desire.
Guests of my gracious memory,
eat of my flesh
and reminiscences,
I want to hear the tearing of bread
between your teeth,
I want to be offered up for the dead!
The land pulses in my veins.
I can feel limestone, phosphorous,
the respite of a root that knows no end.
And this land's saliva finds me out
– a man alone –
like the evergreen lentisk leaf
in the whistling wind that comes off the sea.

It was a green leaf the voyagers remembered.
Sitting on an old wooden fence,
happy to have found the paths where the mockingbird
gave signs of life.

Now I have surrendered to the pleasures
of masts and rigging,
I see absurdity in all things motionless,
like madwomen who laugh at nothing.

Tu olor era la lentitud de la mañana,
y la tibieza de tus senos
motivo de un prolongado silencio.

He soñado con tus grandes extensiones de frescura,
con las sombras que se estremecen
bajo los malecones
y con altos árboles crecidos
bajo la indiferencia de la luna.
Te he soñado viva
entre mis manos
con tu rumor de especies
crepitando,
con los textos divinos
escritos en tus entrañas,
con los despojos
de todo cuanto te es ajeno,
con las flores silvestres que envilecen
los templos y las máscaras.
Te he soñado remontando
la historia de mis palabras
como una yegua overa,
lenta y armoniosa.

Tú, señora de nombre azteca,
fuiste penetrada de ola en ola
por un blanco ejército de gaviotas.

¿Quién como tú?
Quebrantada por el mar
estás ahora,
sepultada en lo profundo de las aguas.

Your scent was the slow, creeping dawn,
and the warmth of your breasts
brought me to an interminable silence.

I have dreamed of your untouched expanses,
where shadows play
below seafront walls
and tall trees grow
under an impassive moon.
I have dreamed
of holding you in my hands, the life
within you and your countless creatures
crackling,
of sacred texts inscribed
in the secret places of your heart
with the remains
of all that is beyond you,
of weeds choking your temples,
defiling the ceremonial masks.
I dreamed I saw you
soaring over this story that I tell,
slow and harmonious
as a dappled mare.

You, woman with an Aztec name,
penetrated by wave after wave
of white armies of gulls.

Who else but you?
Broken into pieces by the sea
and now,
buried in the waters' depths.

Tierra
de toda cosa y todo hombre,
ávida en regiones
y títulos de comarcas.
Tu presencia es mi ley,
tu extensión
la amarra más sagrada.

Tierra,
devuélveme la voz,
deja que mis sueños
sean frecuentados por la verdad
y que la noche se abra
al esplendor del agua.
Despoja de mí
toda historia y condúceme,
tal una colonia de pólipos
o una hambrienta hidra
en busca de la dafnia,
a la memoria del mar divino.

Dios,
que la noche ha roto sus amarras.

Land
to all things and all men
hungry for far-flung territories
and their titles.
Your presence is my governance,
your boundless expanses
my most sacred moorings.

Land,
give me back my voice,
let my dreams
be visited by truths
and let the night open up
to the waters' splendour.
Strip me
of all history, and lead me
like a colony of polyps
or a famished hydra
in search of water-flies,
to the sea's sacred memory.

May God help us,
the night has slipped its moorings.

LECTURA TERCERA

THIRD READING

El sacrificio

Avanzan por el agua las ahogadas.
Buscan la voz del hijo: su única esperanza.
El tiempo, en nubes, las deja inmóviles
bajo el sueño de la noche disipada.

Habíamos perdido nuestras casas.
La gloria de nuestra primera madre.
La fuerza de nuestro primer padre.
Henos aquí, en el Lugar de la Abundancia,
sangrando, gimiendo al sol que gira
y mueve el agua.
Habíamos perdido nuestros nombres,
nuestra primera palabra. De la guerra
y la miseria hicimos la grandeza.
Pintamos todo rostro y todo hueso
al engendrarse el alba.
Abuela, ¿regresaremos a ti?

Pasaron tantos días y tantas noches.
Después el sol, en plena devoción,
penetró la esencia de aquellas Santas.
¡Gritos! ¡Cuántos gritos!
El placer es todo llamas.
Es un infierno donde se ahoga el tiempo. Drown
¡Silencio! Las ahogadas,
cual ramas desprendidas, bailan,
bailan y se abrazan sobre el agua.

The Sacrifice

The drowned women advance in the water
in search of the son's voice: their only hope.
Time, in a cluster of clouds, holds them still
beneath the dream of a dwindling sky.

We had lost our homes.
The glory of our first mother.
The strength of our first father.
And here we were, in the Land of Abundance,[26]
bleeding, groaning at the sun that turns
and moves the waters.
We had lost our names,
our first words. Turned
war and poverty into greatness.
As dawn came forth each day
we painted every face, every bone.
Grandmother, will we ever see you again?

Thus, many days and nights passed.
Then the sun, in hallowed devotion,
penetrated the very souls of the beatified women.
Cries, so many cries went up!
Pleasure is the burning of flames.
A hell where time drowns.
Silence! The drowned women,
like severed branches, dance,
dance and embrace on the water.

Enterradas en la cicatriz del cielo.
Muertas por la conjuración del cielo.
Caídos cormoranes en el charco de los cielos.
Templos.
Maestro Mago,
Maestro Brujo,
«señálanos el camino».
Víboras vírgenes: hálitos.
Llueve luz.
El cielo se abre, pasan
las muchachas, tallan
su olor a líquen.
El cielo arde, brotan
soles,
el día
estalla en gotas de agua.
Maestro Mago,
Maestro Brujo,
Brujito:
«nos duele el cuerpo».
Emigra el día, la noche
es de los árboles.
El mar en sus apariciones
cabalga misterioso
con su máscara de oro.

Tambores.
Retiembla el cielo.
Alzan un corazón,
tierra de agua.
Pasan nubes

Buried in a scarred sky.
Sentenced to death by divine conspiracy.
Fallen cormorants in the heavens' muddy shallows.
Temples.
Great Wise One,
Great Wizard,
Little Wizard:[27]
"show us the way".
Virgin serpents: a breath of air.
Light rains down.
The heavens open
as the young girls file past,
their skin smells of lichens.
The sky burns, shooting out
suns,
daylight
explodes in drops of water.
Great Wise One,
Great Wizard,
Little Wizard:
"our bodies ache".
The day departs, night
settles in the trees.
The sea, in its many guises
rides, mysterious,
wearing a golden mask.

Drums.
The sky throbs.
A heart is held aloft,[28]
land of water.
Clouds drift

del mundo al aire,
del aire anónimas,
retiemblan
los tambores.
La tumba es toda azul.
Alzan un corazón.
Pasan nubes,
lentas,
se desvanecen
sobre el agua.

from land to air,
dissolving into air,
drums
throb.
Death is the colour blue.
A heart is held aloft.
Drifting clouds
slowly pass,
dissolving into air
above the sea.

NOTES

1   The Nahuatl generation myths tell that during the reign of the fourth sun, Chalchiutilicue, the goddess of water, a great flood destroyed the earth and turned men into fish.

2   These three land-based birds were the harbingers of terra firma for the Spanish *conquistadores*, along with the 'rabihorcado', 'black frigate bird' mentioned later in the poem. Christopher Columbus makes particular note of these birds in his account of the days just before reaching land. See entries for 14 September – 4 October in Columbus, *Journal of the First Voyage*, ed. and trans. B.W. Ife (Warminster, England: Aris & Phillips, 1990), pp. 10–22.

3   These lines are a direct quotation from Xavier Villarrutia's "Nocturno de la alcoba" in *Nostalgia de la muerte* (México: Fondo de Cultura Económica, 1984), pp. 66–67. The ultimate message of the poem is that profound intimacy is achieved not through love alone, but in the shared awareness of mortality made possible by love. The final verse reads: 'Then and only then, do we both, alone, know/that it is not love but darkest death/that hastens us to look into each others' eyes,/to reach out and join, more than alone and castaways,/still more, more and more, still.' (Trans. Lorna Shaughnessy).

4   This is the first explicit reference to the fall of Troy. The tone suggests that it follows the Virgilian rather than Homerian tradition. With its enduring images of loss and dispossession, Virgil's *Aeneid* is an important source for *Fábula*.

5   The colour blue is significant in Aztec ritual and myth. The Aztec priests who carried out human sacrifices were painted blue, which was the predominant colour of a principal Aztec god, Huitzilopochtli. It was in honour of Huitzilopochtli that most of the human sacrifices were made. According to legend, he led the Mexica, who we now know as the Aztecs, on a great migration to the site of their great city, Tenochtitlan, the current site of Mexico City. Literally Huitzilopochtli means 'hummingbird on the left' or 'hummingbird of the south'. For the story of his birth and his involvement in the Aztec migration see Walter Krickeberg, *Mitos y leyendas de los aztecas, incas, mayas y muiscas* (México: Fondo de Cultura Económica, 1999, 9th edition), pp. 69–81. For a general discussion of his significance for the Aztecs see the entry for

Huitzilopochtli in Mary Miller and Karl Taube, *An Illustrated Dictionary of The Gods and Symbols of Ancient Mexico and the Maya* (London: Thames and Hudson, 1997), pp. 92–96.

6   Though Hecuba was an aging woman and not a young girl at the fall of Troy, Baranda's image echoes the following scene from *The Aeneid*, Book II: 512–516: 'In the central court, beneath the uncovered sweep of the sky,/Stood a massive altar [...] Here Hecuba and her daughters, like a flock of doves dashed down/By a black storm, were sitting huddled about the altars/That would not protect them, and clasping the images of the gods' – Virgil, *The Aeneid*, trans. C. Day Lewis (Oxford: Oxford University Press, 1986), p. 51

7   This refers to the votive practice in Mexico of pinning to an altar small metallic *ex-votos*, from the Latin for 'from a vow', in anticipation of a prayer answered. The practice is strongly influenced by the pre-Colombian votive tradition.

8   This beautiful image of discovery brings together two distinct moments and traditions: the arrival of the Aztecs to their promised land which was to become the site for of their great city, Tenochtitlan, and the arrival of the Spanish to that very same resplendent city many years later.

9   These are the words of the women in Virgil's *Aeneid* (Book 5, lines 614–615) as they lament their fate seven years after the fall of Troy, wandering in exile, having found no homeland. Deceived by the goddess Iris, they go on to set fire to the boats. Shaughnessy translates the direct quotation Baranda borrows from the Spanish translation of *The Aeneid* in *Virgilio: en verso castellano*, trans. Aurelio Espinosa Pólit (Mexico: Editorial Jus, 1961), p.397.

10 See entries for Saturday, 29 September, and Tuesday 2 October in Columbus, *Journal of the First Voyage, op cit.*, pp. 20–21.

11 Baranda draws this recurring image of drowned women from the belief that the Maya ritually drowned beautiful young virgins in *cenotes*, sacred natural sinkholes, as offerings to appease their gods. The image of the "sagradas doncellas" on page 18 could be such sacrificial virgins. Despite this popular belief, there is no real archaeological evidence that virgins were the principal offering at *cenotes* in the Yucatán peninsula of Mexico, where the remains of the elderly, children, and women have been found.

12 Baranda appears to be paraphrasing God's declaration to Abraham in Genesis 17:7.

13 Shaughnessy translates the direct quotation Baranda makes from the Spanish translation of Virgil's *Georgics*, Book IV: 429–431, *Virgilio en verso castellano, op cit.*, p.403.

14 A dark volcanic glass-like stone, varying from a beautiful olive green to the deepest black. Prized for its lustre and razor-sharp edges, obsidian was the most common material used in ritual instruments for sacrifice and bloodletting. Its mirror-like surface also gave it a central place in divination ceremonies.

15 The *Hail, Holy Queen* is a Catholic Marian antiphon.

16 An edible cactus which is popular in Mexico, where the *nopalitos*, cactus pads, and *tunas*, the 'prickly pear' fruit, are eaten. The nopal is central to Mexican iconography, where legend has it that the Aztecs recognised their promised land when they saw an eagle, with a snake in its mouth, alight on a nopal cactus growing on a mud island in the middle of a lake. The city they founded on that island, Tenochtitlan, means 'place of the cactus' (see notes 5 and 8). The emblem of the eagle on the cactus appears on the Mexican flag and on Mexican metal currency. This bringing together of the olive and the nopal, and their similar shades of green, is characteristic of the way the poem often simultaneously appears to allude to Graeco-Roman, Mesoamaerican and Judeo-Christian traditions and beliefs.

17 Orion, a giant and great hunter, had the power to walk through or on the sea. He was blinded by Oenopion, king of Chios, for raping his daughter Merope. His sight was later returned by the sun god. When Orion saw the Pleiades (the Seven Sisters) he became enamoured, and pursued them. The constellation of Orion appears to still be in pursuit of the Pleiades, who are eternally fleeing west from him. Though it is likely that Baranda is creating a Graeco-Roman mythological context rather than an astrological or cosmological one, the relationship between Orion and the Pleiades is important. The Pleiades were central to Mesoamerican cosmology – for the Aztecs, their ascent to the centre of the sky marked the beginning of a new calendar-round, or 52-year cycle, thus calling for the re-enactment of both the end and beginning of time, and the relevant creation myths. The ensuing cyclical renovation of temples is evident in archaeological remains.

18 There are no tigers in Central America, but *tigre* in Spanish refers to all wild cats, the jaguar in this context. The eagle and the jaguar were the symbols of the two main Aztec military orders. In the archaeological remains in Mexico City of the *teocalli*, the central Aztec temple in Tenochtitlan, painted friezes of the eagle knights

are still visible in the pyramid dedicated to Tlaloc and Huitzilopochtli. The centrality of the eagle and jaguar to military iconography in Central America is not limited to Aztec representations. Painted friezes in the nearby remains of Teotihuacan also represent jaguar knights.

19 In Book IV of *The Georgics*, Virgil turns his attention to bee-keeping. Though he describes the battles between bees in heroic military terms, their epic endeavours are insignificant to man, just as man's epic endeavours are insignificant to Jupiter. In his entreaty to Maecenas, Virgil asserts: "[...] I will show you a spectacle/To marvel at, a world in miniature,/Gallant commanders and the institutions/Of a whole nation, its character, pursuits,/Communities and warfare. Little the scale/To work on, yet not little is the glory/If unpropitious spirits do not cramp/A poet and Apollo hears his prayer." Virgil, *The Georgics*, Book IV: 3–10 (London: Penguin, 1982), trans. L.P. Wilkinson, p.124.

20 This image recalls both the race of humans Prometheus made from clay and the second unsuccessful attempt by the gods in the Mayan *Popol Vuh* to create adequate humans, this time from clay. See note 26 for a discussion of the *Popol Vuh*.

21 These lines are reminiscent of the myth of Orpheus, whose melodic voice drowned the alluring voice of the Sirens so that the Argonauts pass by their rocks unscathed.

22 A Mexican city of arts, not of war, which came under attack from the colonizing Aztecs before the *conquistadores* arrived. Along with Tlaxcala, Texcoco, Atlixco and Tliliuhqui-Tepec, Huexotzinco joined forces with Cortes's army in order to defeat the Aztecs. Although Huexotzinco was an independent city when the Spanish arrived, after defeating the Aztecs the Spanish forced them to pay tributes so high that they faced extinction. See Ross Hassig, *Mexico and the Spanish Conquest* (London: Longman, 1994), pp.20, 71–72, 96, 148.

23 These lines are taken from the Nahuatl poem, "Venimos a soñar" by the 14th century poet, Tochihuitzin Coyolchiuhqui, translated into Spanish by Miguel León de Portilla in *Trece poetas del mundo azteca* (Mexico: UNAM, 1978), p.31 (trans. Lorna Shaughnessy).

24 These lines are a direct quotation from Antonio Machado, "Dos sonetos a Guiomar", *Poesías completas* (Madrid: Ediciones Calpe, Selecciones Austral, 1982, 8th edition), p.360.

25 The Ark of Convenant, when carried in procession, was wrapped in a veil, badger skins, and a blue cloth.

26 These lines are baed on the Quiché Mayan *Popol Vuh* where it recounts the pilgrimage the various Mayan tribes made to the 'Land of Abundance', Tulan, in search of fire. Upon their arrival they realise what they have lost: "'We have forsaken our language. What have we done? We are lost. But where were we misguided? We had only one language when we came from the Place of Abundance [Tulan] we had only one way of worshiping, only one way of living. What we have done is not good,' said all the tribes, beneath the trees, beneath the bushes." Translation by Olwen Rowe from the Spanish, *Popol Vuh*, trans. Asturias y González de Mendoza (Buenos Aires: Losada, 1998), p. 102. The *Popol Vuh*, or the Book of Good Council as it has come to be known in English is central in Mesoamerican culture. It recounts how the gods came to create the 'men of maize', the Mayan peoples. The *Popol Vuh* is comparable with the place the Bible, the Upanishads, or *The Iliad*, *The Odyssey*, and *The Aeneid* have had in their relevant cultures. Originally, the *Popol Vuh* was transmitted orally and visually, through the spoken word and the painted image. In the sixteenth century, it was written down for the first time by a member of the indigenous community in the Mayan language Quiché, with Latin characters.

27 These characters feature in the *Popol Vuh*. Great Wise One and Great Wizard are the hero twins of the *Popol Vuh*, and their escapades dominate the second section of the book. For more information, see Michael D. Coe, *Breaking the Mayan Code* (London: Thames & Hudson, 1999).

28 The sacrifice here seems typically Aztec. However, in the Yucatán peninsula of Mexico, there is archaeological evidence of Mayan ritualistic drowning of sacrificial victims in *cenotes*, sacred natural wells. In the Mayan *Popol Vuh*, the gods repeatedly destroy the beings they create until they create the men of maize who praise them through their words in prayer and also through blood sacrifice, most notably penitential auto-sacrifice, drawing blood from themselves. Although the extraction of the heart from a living victim was rare among the Maya, it did occur. See David Stuart, 'La ideología del sacrificio entre los mayas', *Arqueología mexicana*, 2003: XI (63), pp. 24–29.

APC 2012: Your practical guide to success

GW00982560

Christina Hirst

RICS
the mark of
property
professionalism
worldwide

Published by the Royal Institution of Chartered Surveyors (RICS)
Surveyor Court
Westwood Business Park
Coventry CV4 8JE
UK
www.ricsbooks.com

First edition published 2001
Second edition published 2003, reprinted 2005
Third edition published 2006
Fourth edition published 2009
Fifth edition published 2010

ISBN 978 1 84219 688 5

Typeset in Great Britain by Columns Design XML Ltd, Reading, Berks

Printed in Great Britain by Page Bros, Norwich

Contents

Contents

Contents

Preface

Like its previous editions the aim of this book is to guide you through your APC from the very beginning of your structured training to your success at final assessment. I would like make clear that the objective of this book is not to replace the RICS formal guidance but to supplement this. The APC by its very nature must be dynamic and must adapt to reflect changes in the work and practice of surveyors; therefore, you should ensure that you follow the up to date guidance published by RICS at www.rics.org/apc. The contact details page at the back of the book will help point you in the right direction for this and other formal information.

I have been involved with the APC as an RICS training adviser for over ten years now and during that time have met many different candidates working in a vast range of organisations. There are a number of useful tips that all candidates seem to agree on:

- Keep up to date with your APC diary and templates.

- Make sure you understand the requirements from the outset.

- Manage your supervisor and counsellor!

- Ask if you are not sure – the hardest question to answer is the one that starts 'this may be a daft question…'!

This book will help you address these and more.

The APC pathways and competencies have been developed and agreed by practising surveyors within the different professional groups. They are intended to reflect the work of surveyors within the particular specialisms. Generally you will find that your day to day work will allow you to meet the necessary competencies but if you feel this would be difficult to achieve discuss this with your supervisor and counsellor when agreeing your training plan. There are many different ways that additional experience can be obtained, including working with others in your organisation or taking a secondment. You should never feel that it is not possible to succeed in your APC – where there is a will there is a way.

I would urge you to project manage your APC. Take time out to set an action plan for yourself and set time aside each week to do your diary much in the same way as you will have set time aside for your studies. Think of the APC as a qualification – little and often is usually a good approach to studying. Don't leave everything until the very end – choose your critical analysis project early and use your professional development to help you to develop the necessary additional knowledge you may need.

The APC will take time and effort but the rewards are immense – chartered surveyors truly are the gold standard in the property and construction professions. Good luck with your APC and best wishes for a long, prosperous and successful surveying career.

Christina Hirst

1 APC overview

This chapter provides an overview of the basic philosophies and key concepts of the APC, as well as an introduction to the guidance documents and templates and a note of relevant dates and deadlines. It also outlines the roles and responsibilities of some of the people essential to your training and development, such as RICS training advisers (RTAs), APC doctors, your employer and RICS itself.

Routes to membership

There are various 'routes' that will lead you to chartered membership of RICS, including:

- **Graduate route 1** – for those with an RICS accredited degree and less than five years relevant surveying experience;

- **Graduate route 2** – for those with an RICS accredited degree and between five and ten years relevant surveying experience (this may include pre-degree experience);

- **Graduate route 3** – for those with an RICS accredited degree and ten-years or more relevant surveying experience (this may include pre-degree experience);

- **Adaptation route** – for those with either an RICS approved professional body membership or non-accredited but relevant degree and nine years relevant surveying experience. Candidates for this route must complete 450 study hours from an RICS accredited degree either at postgraduate level, from the final year of an undergraduate degree or from an approved training provider;

- **Academic** – for those who hold a surveying related higher degree and have undertaken academic activities on an RICS accredited degree over a three year period or who hold an RICS accredited degree and have undertaken academic activities relating to the profession over a three year period; and

- **Senior professional** – for professionals who are now in a senior industry position and hold a surveying related degree and have more than five years surveying experience.

- **Professional experience route** – for graduate professionals with five years or more relevant post graduate experience.

Linked to the routes are a series of APC 'pathways' and before you begin the APC you must choose, in consultation with your employer, an APC pathway appropriate to the work experience you will be able to obtain. The pathway chosen will lead you to membership of one of the RICS professional groups and many will give you the opportunity to use an alternative designation in addition to the title 'Chartered Surveyor', for example, Chartered Building Surveyor if you take the building surveying pathway.

This book aims to guide you along graduate routes 1 and 2, although chapter 5 will also be useful for candidates on graduate route 3.

Official guidance

This book does not intend to repeat the contents of the RICS APC guidance. It is therefore essential that you read and study the guidance available at www.rics.org/apc. You should also be aware that this book focuses on version 2/December 2008 of the APC guidance; however, you must keep up to date with any changes that are published by RICS and, most importantly, watch out for any transitional arrangements that may occur. Guidance is provided for candidates, supervisors, counsellors and employers with the aim of helping candidates through the APC and helping employers support their candidates. Above all, for employers the guidance outlines the commitment needed – it is important that your employer not only has a copy of the guidance, but is fully aware of their responsibilities. You might like to give them a little encouragement to read it!

The RICS APC Pathways Guides have been written by experienced practitioners and aim to give a clear and practical understanding of how to apply the listed core and optional competencies in the context of your specific pathway and area of work. The official competency definitions (at levels one, two and three) are provided, followed by a description of the key knowledge and activities that are likely to fall within the scope of each competency. An example is provided in chapter 2 on page 22.

What is the APC?

The Assessment of Professional Competence (APC) is the process by which RICS seeks to be satisfied that candidates who wish to become members of the Institution are competent to practise as chartered surveyors.

To demonstrate this competence, candidates will undergo a rigorous and demanding period of structured training, over a minimum period of 23 calendar months, in which they must gain a minimum of 400 days of relevant work experience as well as undertake additional professional development. (For graduate route 2 candidates, the minimum requirement is 11 months and 200 days of relevant experience.) The objective is to enable the knowledge and theory gained primarily in higher education to be complemented by practical experience. The second part of the APC process is then the final assessment interview. The APC therefore comprises of two components:

1   *a period of structured training*: during this period you should keep a record, in a diary, of experience gained. You must also keep a candidate achievement record (see page 80) and an experience record (see page 81). The training period also incorporates your professional development, an outline of which is given later in this chapter (see also page 9);

2   *the final assessment interview*: a panel of a minimum of two assessors (although this panel will normally comprise of three practitioners) will interview you over a period of one hour, and form a judgment, or 'assess', whether you are competent to practise as a member of RICS. (See chapter 5.)

You should think of the APC as the practical training and experience which, when added to the study normally carried out at university, leads to membership of RICS (illustrated by figure 1).

The APC can commence at a number of points depending upon your circumstances. For a graduate route 1 candidate you can start APC:

- after you have graduated from an RICS accredited degree;

- at the beginning of a 'year out' placement from an RICS accredited sandwich degree;

- at the beginning of the final year of a part time or distance learning RICS accredited undergraduate degree; or

- at the beginning of the penultimate year of a part time or distance learning RICS accredited post graduate degree.

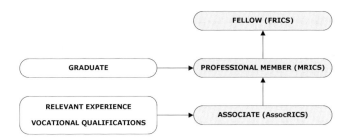

Figure 1 Route to membership of RICS

The starting points for graduate route 2 candidates are often later as you will already have more than 5 years experience on starting the APC. The 11 month period of structured training for graduate route 2 must start after you have graduated unless you are taking an accredited part time post graduate degree where this can commence at the beginning of the final year.

The APC is a process of continuous assessment culminating in the final assessment by the RICS panel of assessors. Many candidates tend to focus on the final assessment only but you must firstly satisfy your supervisor and counsellor of your competence before you are able to go forward to the final assessment. At the final assessment the panel will consider:

- the depth and breadth of your training;

- the quality of your documents and written reports (including the critical analysis and candidate experience record); and

- your presentation at the interview.

At the end of the interview the panel will view your training and development with a holistic view of performance.

Key concepts and documents

Competent to practise

The APC is foremost a period of structured training and practical experience, which culminates in the final assessment interview, the objective of which is to assess your 'competence to practise', in other words your competence to carry out the work of a qualified surveyor. To be 'competent' is to have the skill or knowledge to carry out a task or function successfully. This ability can vary from being merely able, to being expert in a particular sphere of activity.

The APC requires you to achieve various competencies relevant to your APC pathway. The competencies are a mix of technical, professional and personal skills and come in three different categories:

1   mandatory competencies;

2   core competencies; and

3   optional competencies.

As you progress through the APC you will need to demonstrate to your supervisor and counsellor, and ultimately the final assessment panel, that you meet the knowledge requirements of your chosen pathway. In addition, you will need to demonstrate the practical application of this knowledge and the ability to solve problems. You will also need to show that you have been developing the range of knowledge and skills required in the mandatory competencies, which comprise a mix of professional practice and interpersonal, business and management skills that are considered common to, and necessary for, all surveyors.

You will note that, most importantly, there is a focus on testing that you are aware of and intend to act in accordance with the RICS Rules of Conduct and that you understand the importance of ethics and professional practice matters. There is a specific guidance note on the Rules of Conduct for APC candidates, supervisors and counsellors further reinforcing the importance of this area. This is available at www.rics.org/apc

A competency

A competency is a statement of the skills or abilities required to perform a specific task or function. It is based upon attitudes and behaviours, as well as skills and knowledge. For the APC, the requirements and level of attainment for each pathway are set out in the APC guidance. Chapter 2 provides details of specific competencies and shows how, at the final assessment, these will be drawn together by the assessment panel to form a holistic judgment of your competence to practise.

Structured training

'Structured training' is, as its name suggests, a structured approach to the delivery of training and experience over a given period. It is mandatory for all firms registering new APC candidates to have an approved structured training agreement in place. A template for use by employers in developing a structured training agreement can be downloaded from www.rics.org/apc

The structured training agreement is an agreement between your employer and RICS that formalises your employer's intended policy in implementing the RICS requirements for the APC. You will find more detail on this document in chapter 2.

There is no minimum requirement of training days to be completed under each competency, other than the overall requirement of the structured training period. For graduate route 1 this is a minimum of 400 days within

23 calendar months and for graduate route 2 this is a minimum of 200 days within 11 calendar months.

There is no specified period of structured training for graduate route 3.

An employer's structured training agreement must be approved by RICS. Once approved by your, your employer will be listed on www.rics.org as having an approved structured training agreement.

APC templates

All the templates you will need for your APC are available on the RICS website (www.rics.org/apc). With the exception of the diary template these are all included within an Excel workbook for your specific pathway.

Diary

The diary (see page 78) is a day-to-day record of how you have been building your experience. The detail contained in it will assist you in completing your candidate achievement record and your experience record.

Candidate achievement record

The candidate achievement record (see page 80) includes what is known as the log book.

In this record you will give a monthly summary of the entries in your diary and provide a total of the number of days of experience gained in each of the competencies.

The candidate achievement record also charts your progress against the competency requirements of your chosen pathway using the log book summary. In other words, it is a record of your competency achievements as assessed by your supervisor and counsellor.

Professional development

Another important aspect of the training period is the requirement for you to undertake a minimum of 48 hours of professional development per annum. This is to provide you with the opportunity to gain knowledge and skills that might not be available in your day-to-day training environment and may be used to complement the requirements of the mandatory competencies. Professional development is recorded in the professional development record. Information recorded includes the date of the activity, the subject, the number of hours and the type of professional development (personal, technical or professional).

In the context of your career, your professional development never ends. When you have completed your professional development for APC purposes, RICS then requires you, as a member, to undertake lifelong learning, or continuing professional development (CPD) as it is sometimes known thereafter. The concept of professional development for the APC is explored in more detail in chapter 2.

Change of employer

If you change employer during the training period you should continue your records in the usual way, but there must be a clear note of the change of employer. In particular, the new position regarding your supervisor and/or counsellor must be indicated for the purposes of certification at the final assessment. RICS must also be advised of the change of employer using the 'change of employer form' available at www.rics.org/apc. RICS will record the change or detail the action you need to take to resolve any problems.

Important dates and deadlines – a chronology of the APC

Now that we have reviewed some of the key concepts and documents for the APC, we will take a brief look at some of the important dates and deadlines that you will need to adhere to during the training period.

Enrolment

A delay of a few weeks in your enrolment could put your final assessment back six months, as final assessments are normally held only twice a year. Closing dates are given on www.rics.org/apc where you will also find detailed support.

The enrolment form is available from the RICS Contact Centre. You must send the enrolment form, completed by yourself and your employer with the correct fee, to RICS Membership Operations. Details of the fees are included with the enrolment form. You must submit all the required material otherwise your enrolment cannot be accepted.

Once accepted, RICS will confirm your registration and give you a start date for recording your experience. You will be able to backdate your experience for one month from your enrolment date.

Acknowledgment by RICS

RICS will confirm your registration and give you a date from which you may start recording your experience. Don't forget the importance of this date, as before you reach the final assessment, if you are a graduate route 1 candidate, you will need to have completed a minimum of 400 days' experience within 23 calendar months (for a graduate route 2 candidate you will need to have completed 200 days' experience within 11 months).

To be considered for either a session 1 or 2 assessment in a given year, you must have completed the required minimum training period. It follows, therefore, that a delay of a few weeks in enrolling could put the assessment date back by six months. You will need to decide your target final assessment date with your supervisor and counsellor. All the assessment information is available at www.rics.org/apc

Three-monthly reviews by your supervisor

Every three months your supervisor will discuss and review your progress against the competencies and you will complete the candidate achievement record and experience record.

Six-monthly reviews by your counsellor

At six-monthly intervals your counsellor will discuss and review your progress against the competencies and you will complete the candidate achievement record and experience record. Your counsellor's assessment constitutes a second opinion to that of the supervisor and will be completed in consultation with you and your supervisor.

Final assessment

It is your responsibility to keep all key dates in your work schedule. All the assessment information is available at www.rics.org/apc. You will have decided your target final assessment date with your supervisor and counsellor and you will need to send in the completed application form within the dates specified on the RICS website. You will then have approximately one month to submit the required documents for the final assessment presentation and interview. Details of the required documents can be found on www.rics.org/apc

Results

RICS will send your results by first class post 21 days after your interview. It is your responsibility to check RICS has your up to date address. You will receive either a pass or a referral. If you are successful you will be awarded professional membership of RICS (MRICS). If you receive a referral you will be informed of the next steps to be taken. For security and data protection reasons, RICS will not give results over the telephone, by fax, email or to a third party.

Appeals

An appeal, if appropriate, should be received by RICS no later than ten days from the date of your result letter. Details of how to make an appeal are on www.rics.org/apc

When an appeal is made it must:

- be in writing, accompanied by the appropriate fee;

- be made by you and not a third party; and

- clearly state the grounds on which the appeal is being made, supported by appropriate evidence.

Finding help

Completing the APC carries with it a lot of responsibility and commitment. Both support and guidance are available for candidates and employers and for many queries you can contact RICS (see page 165).

There are also others who are there to help you and your employer with your APC, including:

- your employer, your supervisor and your counsellor;

- APC doctors;

- RICS regional training advisers (RTA); and

- other candidates (perhaps by way of the APC Discussion Forum).

Your employer, your supervisor and your counsellor

Now that we have considered the key concepts behind the APC you will see that this is not something you can do on your own. Your employer will play a critical role in your APC both in the context of providing you with the necessary structured training and in assessing your progress against the competencies.

It may be that you have been working for your employer for some time before starting the APC or you may be specifically seeking employment that will support you through this. Either way you may be considering how you can ensure that your employer will be able to provide you with the support you need. Some questions you should consider are:

- Is the employer listed on the RICS website as having an approved structured training agreement?

- Does the employer have a proven track record of training APC candidates? Does the employer have its own schemes for providing professional development?

- Does the employer have Investor in People accreditation? The Investor in People standard is given to firms who set high standards in terms of their commitment to, and their planning, delivery and evaluation of training and development for their staff.

- How does the employer plan to assist you in meeting the competency requirements? Can everything be done in-house? Will you be moved between departments or offices? Are secondments or exchanges available with other firms to make up any shortfalls? In addition, you might like to ask if you can speak to any of the firm's current or recent APC candidates.

- Who will be your supervisor and counsellor, and what is their experience of the APC?

Patience and understanding is also recommended. Most candidates have an expectation of being ready for the final assessment as soon as the minimum training period of 400 days within 23 calendar months (for graduate route 1) has elapsed. This is not always possible and sometimes, because of business practicalities or priorities, your employer may not have been able to give you the full spread of training against the competencies. Alternatively, you may not have progressed against certain competencies as quickly as expected. Don't forget, we all develop at different speeds in any of life's skills.

You should only apply for your final assessment when you, your supervisor and your counsellor feel you are ready and are confident that you have gained the necessary training and experience – even if that means that your training period lasts for 30, or even 36, months. Be prepared to cooperate with your employer and, most importantly, listen to the advice of your supervisor and counsellor.

While you will develop certain expectations concerning your APC training, your employer will also be looking for a return from you by way of hard work, enterprise and fee income! You will need to approach the partnership with your employer with a degree of understanding and awareness, giving careful thought as to how you will balance the demands of your employer with your own need to make progress with the APC.

Finally, the importance of the employer cannot be overemphasised in terms of the appointment of your supervisor and counsellor, who are usually part of your employer's team. Your supervisor and counsellor will act as guides and mentors throughout and, in many instances, beyond your training period and their roles will be of particular importance during preparation for your final assessment. It is important that this is an active partnership, where the employer takes a proactive approach, by way of interest and involvement, in your training and development.

It is sometimes said that it is only large firms who can provide the best opportunities for APC training and that small firms may struggle. However, a small firm with a varied portfolio of work can provide more than adequate training and experience for APC candidates.

So, do not be slow in coming forward; it's in your own best interest to find an employer who will provide you with the training and experience you need to ensure that success at the final assessment interview is a formality. But do not lose sight of the fact that you are entering into a partnership and that your employer will also want a return on the investment.

RICS training advisers (RTAs)

RICS employs training advisers for each region in the UK. Details may be found on the RICS website at www.rics.org/apc

The role of an RTA is to advise employers on all aspects of the APC. Most importantly, they help firms develop structured training agreements (see chapter 2 for more information). In drawing up such an agreement the RTA will provide advice to your employer. When your employer has prepared a training agreement that meets with the minimum standards, it can be approved by RICS and used as an indicator of excellence and of the firm's commitment to APC training.

You should encourage your employer to discuss the structured training agreement and any APC training issues they may have with the local RTA.

APC doctors

Whereas the primary role of the RTAs is to support and advise employers, voluntary APC doctors are available to assist and guide candidates through the system. They are normally locally based and, where practical, will be from the same professional group as your own. They are often recently successful APC candidates and can therefore provide others with the benefit of their first-hand experience. Details of local APC doctors can be found on www.rics.org/apc

Reading material

There is a wealth of reading material and information available from www.ricsbooks.com. You may find it particularly useful to use the RICS online knowledge resource for property professionals – *isurv* (www.isurv.com). The *isurv* 'channels' cover a huge range of surveying topics, mixing expert commentary with official RICS guidance. The *isurv* APC channel also holds excellent support material (www.isurv.com/apc).

Other candidates

Sharing ideas and approaches with other candidates can be an excellent way to find answers to queries and to gain advice. This might be through your local RICS Matrics group, through local events or perhaps by way of the APC Discussion Forum on the RICS website.

Summary

- It is essential to read the APC guidance available at www.rics.org/apc

- For graduate route 1 you will need to complete a minimum two-year period (400 days within a minimum of 23 calendar months) of training and practical experience.

- For graduate route 2 the minimum period is 200 days within 11 calendar months.

- It is important that you have a clear picture of what is meant by the term 'competent to practise', with regard to knowledge; problem-solving abilities; business and practice skills; personal and interpersonal skills; and the Rules of Conduct and professional ethics.

- A structured training agreement must be completed by your employer.

- Training and practical experience culminates in the final assessment: a one-hour interview with a panel of three (sometimes two) experienced practitioners, who will consider whether you are 'competent to practise'.

- Information and evidence of training and experience must be kept in your diary, candidate achievement record and experience record.

- You must undertake a minimum of 48 hours of professional development for every 12 months of training completed.

- If you change employer, you must notify RICS.

- RICS will give you a start date for recording your experience.

- All assessment information is available on www.rics.org/apc. You will have decided your target final assessment date with your supervisor.

- Results will be sent by first class post 21 days after your interview. If you are referred and wish to appeal, you must do so no later than 10 days from the date of your results letter.

- Help with the APC is available from RICS and APC doctors.

- Help for your employer is available from RTAs.

- Remember the APC is all about a partnership between yourself and your employer.

2 The training period

This chapter looks at how to go about managing your training period. It aims to develop your understanding of the competencies and illustrate how professional development can be used as a tool to assist your progress. Structured training will be considered in some detail, with particular regard to the various templates that need to be completed.

The pathways

There are 21 pathways available in the APC, recognising the diversity of the surveying profession. The pathways are set out on the RICS website www.rics.org/apc. In consultation with your supervisor and your counsellor you should choose the pathway that best suits the work you are, and will be, involved in during the course of your APC. While it is important to consider your career aspirations when making your choice of pathway, you cannot achieve the requirements unless you gain relevant experience. The experience available to you in your firm should steer your choice.

You should also remember that the pathway through which you qualify may give you the right to use an alternative designation in addition to 'Chartered Suryeyor'. This may be important for you and for future employers. The RICS Contact Centre can provide further advice regarding alternative designations.

The competencies

A key aspect to the successful management of the training period is an in-depth knowledge and understanding of the competencies and requirements of each RICS professional group, which are contained in the appropriate APC pathway. Further guidance on the pathways is available at www.rics.org/apc

Chapter 1 discussed the meaning of 'competent' and explored what is meant by a competency. In the broader context, the use of competency-based training and, most importantly, competency-based interviewing, is fast becoming a worldwide phenomenon. As your career progresses and develops, you will find that your appreciation of this subject will grow. However, at this stage it is important that you fully understand competencies in the context of your APC. The advice that follows is therefore tailored to fit that particular need.

The APC guidance sets out what you need to achieve by way of skills and abilities over the training period. It indicates the specific competency requirements of each pathway, with guidelines on the number of competencies to be covered during the training period, and the depth and level of attainment required.

The competency choices must be made in consultation and with the agreement of your counsellor and supervisor and must reflect the work you carry out in your day-to-day environment. This choice will be considered as a reflection of your judgment at the final assessment. The APC guidance on each pathway will give a further insight into the experience requirements.

For some pathways the achievement of competencies at a certain level can be important for your future work. For example if you intend to undertake Red Book Valuations you will need to become a member of the RICS Valuer

Registration Scheme. Members who qualify on or after 1 October 2011 will only be eligible to join if they have qualified at APC final assessment with competency in valuation to level 3.

Members who have not qualified at the appropriate level in valuation will be registered on the Scheme on a probationary basis for six months to gain supervised experience, after which they will be required to be assessed in the valuation competency at level 3.

The APC guidance also sets out the full list of competencies in alphabetical order, with a reference for each – for example, Inspection T044. This reference number is for use on your candidate achievement record and your experience record.

The competencies are varied and cover a wide range of technical, professional practice, business, management and interpersonal skills. For each competency, there are three levels of attainment:

- **Level 1** – knowledge and understanding of the areas covered by the competency;

- **Level 2** – application of this knowledge and understanding in normal practical situations; and

- **Level 3** – ability to provide reasoned advice and depth of technical knowledge.

Consider the example below of the building surveying competency of 'building pathology', which progresses in complexity across the levels.

> *Building pathology*
>
> **Level 1:** demonstrate your knowledge and understanding of building defects including collection of information, measurements and tests.
>
> **Level 2:** apply your knowledge to undertake surveys, use survey and other information to diagnose cause and mechanisms of failure.
>
> **Level 3:** provide evidence of reasoned advice and appropriate recommendations, including the preparation and presentation of reports.
>
> A typical final assessment question for this competency might be:
>
> 'I notice from your experience record that you have carried out building surveys on a number of traditionally built 1960s houses. Describe how you went about those surveys [level 1]. What were the common types of failure to brickwork observed while carrying out those inspections? What were the causes and how did you diagnose these? [level 2]. If you identified diagonal cracking in brickwork of houses of this age with basements what might cause this and what method of repair would you recommend to your client, and why? What sort of issues would you include in your final report and recommendations? [level 3].'

The guidance on pathways further illuminates the experience requirements within each of the competencies. Set out overleaf is an explanation of the experience required in the building pathology competency taken from the building surveying pathway guidance.

Building pathology

Level 1: Demonstrate knowledge and understanding of:

- typical defects relating to typical buildings found in your locality that you may have come across and explain cause and effect of these;
- building defects likely to be encountered in typical building surveying activities, for example, wet and dry rot, flat roof defects and concrete defects;
- the various methods to collect, store and retrieve information for various differing purposes when carrying out property inspections;
- the various different types of inspection that may be carried out and the importance of accurate recording of information during inspection; and
- differing types of testing and the limitations of the tests, for example, the use of damp meters and borescopes.

Level 2:

- explain in detail cause and mechanics of varying types of failure;
- explain procedures for carrying out inspections of properties;
- be able to explain, using detailed examples, the relationship between observations taken on site and the diagnosis of failure in building fabric;
- be able to use examples, from your own experience, to demonstrate your application of knowledge gained at level 1; and
- be able to use knowledge and information gathered from several sources, including, if necessary, specialist inspections to diagnose and explain building fabric failure.

Level 3:

- prepare reports for clients, explaining in non-technical language the causes of failure and the likely results of failure, together with the appropriate remedial measures;

- using information gathered from inspections formulate the necessary remedial/preventative works including specific detail in the form of a schedule of works if required;

- show an understanding of the level of detail required in typical reports, including examples of layout and the use of sketches, drawings and photographs;

- be able to discuss in detail examples of unusual defects you have been involved with and remedial works employed; and

- be able to demonstrate the differing requirements of reports to clients, for example, the differences between schedules of condition, schedules of dilapidations and pre-acquisition reports.

You will reach these levels in a logical progression and in successive stages. There is no minimum number of days of training required to achieve a particular level of attainment in any of the competencies. In discussion with your supervisor and counsellor, a decision will be made as to when you have reached the required level of skill and ability in any particular competency. The number of days taken to reach the appropriate level will be dependent upon a combination of the following factors:

- your starting point – have you had any previous experience?;

- your aptitude and speed of learning in the competency;

- the quality of the training and experience given by the employer; and

- the particular competency – is it merely measurement, or nuclear physics?

For some candidates who already have experience prior to starting the APC some levels of competencies may be achieved from the outset. The judgment as to your achievement will be made by your supervisor and counsellor, who will then confirm this, and you will be able to update your candidate achievement record accordingly.

Each pathway requires you to satisfy three types of competency:

1 mandatory competencies;

2 core competencies; and

3 optional competencies.

The mandatory competencies generally relate to professional practice, interpersonal, management and business skills and are common to all pathways. The core competencies relate to the primary skills of your chosen pathway. The optional competencies are selected by you from a list contained in the APC guidance for the appropriate pathway.

The mandatory competencies – outline

The minimum standards for mandatory competencies are set out in the APC guidance and are structured in levels. You must achieve the minimum standards, as follows:

• Conduct rules, ethics and professional practice	Level 3
• Client care • Communication and negotiation • Health and safety	Level 2

• Accounting principles and procedures • Business planning • Conflict avoidance, management and dispute resolution procedures • Data management • Sustainability • Teamworking	Level 1

All of the above competencies are defined in the APC guidance.

The minimum standards described above may also be included at a higher level, if appropriate to the particular pathway. If a pathway includes a mandatory competency to a higher level, this will also appear in the core or optional competency list for that pathway, to the higher level.

Overall, when your employer develops your structured training agreement, they will need to set out how you will achieve the required mandatory, core and optional competencies. Your employer will identify the mandatory competencies where you will receive the appropriate training within your day-to-day work, as part of your structured training. This will leave you with a remainder which may require you to undertake additional learning, a specific training course or gain further experience. These actions may qualify for your professional development.

The mandatory competencies – in detail

The mandatory competencies are one of the most important parts of the APC. The skills and abilities they encourage and test underpin all professional and technical aspects of working as a surveyor, and are vital for further advancement in the profession.

This chapter will give some further explanation of the requirements for each competency and provide some practical advice on how to help you achieve the required levels, working through the levels outlined.

The advice is not intended to be all-encompassing, or definitive in any way – each candidate, each pathway, and each firm will alter the ingredients of each competency slightly. It is certainly not possible to say, 'follow this, and you will pass'. What follows are suggestions and pointers as to how the requirements of the competencies might be met.

In particular, you should note that the recommended reading is not exhaustive – it is, in the main, a selection of some books and texts that candidates have found useful. Each pathway will have its own specialist authors and texts, and you should talk to your supervisor and counsellor, asking for their views and recommendations based on their experience, which should be more tailored to your pathway.

Some of the training suggested for the mandatory competencies – particularly the structured reading – may also prove useful for professional development purposes. Remember that some 32 hours of professional development a year must be focused around the areas of the mandatory competencies (16 hours on mandatory competencies and a further 16 hours on professional practice). In particular, you may wish to use the RICS online knowledge resource for property professionals – *isurv* (www.isurv.com). This service, mixing expert commentary with official RICS guidance, covers a huge range of surveying matters, and can be used for professional development purposes.

The minimum requirements for the competencies in the mandatory competency list vary from level 1 to level 3. Where a competency is required to a level higher than 1, I will explain how to move from one level to the next.

Remember it is important to achieve the required levels in a progressive manner. You cannot just achieve level 3 from a standing start so it is important that you understand the requirements at each level.

For each of the competencies discussed you should refer to the APC guidance for the detailed definitions. The following sections simply provide further practical guidance to support these definitions.

Conduct rules, ethics and professional practice

This competency is arguably the most important of all. In order to be successful in the APC final assessment you must demonstrate your awareness of and intention to act within the RICS Rules of Conduct for both members and firms. The Rules of Conduct are critical to the profession for it is these and the underpinning values that give confidence to the public and our clients that we are a 'safe pair of hands' and that we are regulated by our professional body. Unsurprisingly, this competency must be achieved to level 3.

Let's take a look at some key concepts.

Being a professional

As a professional body RICS has a responsibility to protect the public by ensuring its members operate to the highest ethical standard. RICS is incorporated by Royal Charter, which sets out the objects of the Institution and requires it to:

> 'maintain and promote the usefulness of the profession for the public advantage.'

Therefore, to practise as a member of RICS at any level, you must prove that you are ethically sound. Before introducing the RICS standards, it is worth considering what a professional is.

Key personal qualities of a professional include ability, confidence, responsibility, belief and respect, honour, reputation and trustworthiness.

A definition of professionalism was given by Howard Land FRICS in *Professional ethics and the Rules of Conduct of the RICS* (College of Estate Management, 1997):

> 'Professionalism is the giving of one's best to ensure that clients' interests are properly cared for, but in doing so the wider public interest is also recognised and respected.'

Professionals show high levels of ethical responsibility, ethics being defined as the 'science of morals'. As a branch of philosophy ethics is concerned with theories of goodness and badness or right and wrong and of morality.

In recent years additional focus has been placed on ethics and many have called for more openness and transparency in business dealings. Traditional business problems cannot always be resolved by legislation and experience, hence the need for professional institutions to develop their own ethical codes.

RICS Rules of Conduct

Professional ethics are monitored by RICS Regulation, with reference to the Rules of Conduct. The Rules of Conduct for members are principles-based and are clear and simple rules that adopt the five principles of good regulation:

1 Proportionality

2 Accountability

3 Consistency

4 Targeting

5 Transparency

The Rules position RICS as a bold, cutting-edge professional regulator for the 21st century.

The Rules of Conduct for members cover those matters for which individual members are responsible and accountable in their professional lives. They apply equally to all members, wherever they are in the world and whatever their chosen field of activity. There are also a series of help sheets on different aspects of the rules.

- Members shall at all times act with integrity and avoid conflicts of interest and any actions or situations that are inconsistent with their professional obligations

- Members shall carry out their professional work with due skill, care and diligence and with proper regard for the technical standards expected of them.

- Members shall carry out their professional work in a timely manner and with proper regard for standards of service and customer care expected of them.

- Members shall plan, undertake, record and evaluate appropriate continuing professional development and, on request, provide RICS with evidence that they have done so.

- Members shall ensure that their personal and professional finances are managed appropriately.

- Members shall submit in a timely manner such information, and in such form, as the Regulatory Board may reasonably require.

- Members shall cooperate fully with RICS staff and any person appointed by the Regulatory Board.

There are also Rules of Conduct for firms. These rules set out the standards of professional conduct and practice expected of firms registered for regulation by RICS.

- A Firm shall at all times act with integrity and avoid conflicts of interest and any actions or situations that are inconsistent with its professional obligations.

- A Firm shall carry out its professional work with due skill, care and diligence and with proper regard for the technical standards expected of it.

- A Firm shall carry out its professional work with expedition and with proper regard for standards of service and customer care expected of it.

- A Firm shall have in place the necessary procedures to ensure that all its staff are properly trained and competent to do their work.

- A Firm shall operate a complaints handling procedure. The complaints handling procedure must include a redress mechanism that is approved by the Regulatory Board.

- A Firm shall preserve the security of clients' money entrusted to its care in the course of its practice or business.

- A Firm shall ensure that all previous and current professional work is covered by adequate and appropriate professional indemnity insurance cover which meets standards approved by the Regulatory Board.

- A Firm shall promote its professional services only in a truthful and responsible manner.

- A Firm shall ensure that its finances are managed appropriately.

- A Firm that has a sole principal (i.e. a sole practitioner or a sole director in a corporate practice) shall have in place appropriate arrangements in the event of that sole principal's death or incapacity or other extended absences.

- A Firm registered for regulation must display on its business literature, in accordance with the Regulatory Board's published policy on designations, a designation to denote that it is regulated by RICS.

- A Firm shall submit in a timely manner such information about its activities, and in such form, as the Regulatory Board may reasonably require.

- A Firm shall cooperate fully with RICS staff and any person appointed by the Regulatory Board.

More about these ethical standards, together with useful guidance, can be found at www.rics.org/regulation

Level 1

The knowledge and understanding required of the candidate at level 1 is wide-ranging. It covers the role, function and significance of RICS; an understanding of society's expectations of professional practice; RICS Rules of Conduct for both firms and members; and the general principles of law and the legal system, as applicable in your area of practice.

The RICS Rules of Conduct, policies and associated helpsheets are available on www.rics.org/regulation. You should make sure that you are aware of the rules for both members and firms.

To understand the role and function of RICS, you should carry out some reading around the structure of RICS, the various professional groups, group boards and committees, and the functions performed, such as advising the government on housing, taxation, planning and landlord and tenant issues and bringing an influence to bear on all relevant aspects of society. Apart from keeping abreast of developments in newspapers, a good source of information is the RICS magazine, *Modus*, and the various other RICS journals and 'property' publications.

The other requirement at level 1 involves the candidate understanding the role of the professional person and of society's expectations of such a person. The general principles of professional integrity (the 12 standards listed below) hold good in all professional-client situations. An important issue is that of 'ethics', which have been defined as a set of moral principles extending beyond a formal code of conduct.

RICS expects members to act both within the Rules of Conduct and to maintain professional and ethical standards. Members are expected to apply a set of 12 standards in order to meet the high standards of behaviour expected of them. These standards are to:

- Act honourably – Never put your own gain above the welfare of your clients or others to whom you have a professional responsibility. Always consider the wider interests of society in your judgments.

- Act with integrity – Be trustworthy in all that you do – never deliberately mislead, whether by withholding or distorting information.

- Be open and transparent in your dealings – Share the full facts with your clients, making things as plain and intelligible as possible.

- Be accountable for all your actions – Take full responsibility for your actions and don't blame others if things go wrong.

- Know and act within your limitations – Be aware of the limits of your competence and don't be tempted to work beyond these. Never commit to more than you can deliver.

- Be objective at all times – Give clear and appropriate advice. Never let sentiments or your own interests cloud your judgment.

- Always treat others with respect – Never discriminate against others.

- Set a good example – Remember that both your public and private behaviour could affect your own, RICS' and other members' reputations.

- Have the courage to make a stand – Be prepared to act if you suspect a risk to safety or malpractice of any sort.

- Comply with relevant laws and regulations – Avoid any action, illegal or litigious, that may bring the profession into disrepute.

- Avoid conflicts of interest – Declare any potential conflicts of interest, personal or professional, to all relevant parties.

- Respect confidentiality – Maintain the confidentiality of your clients' affairs. Never divulge information to others unless it is necessary.

Level 2

Level 2 in this competency requires you to provide evidence of practical application in your area of practice, being able to justify actions at all times and demonstrate personal commitment to the Rules of Conduct, ethics and the twelve standards.

Level 3

At level 3, you should be able to provide evidence of the application of the above in your area of practice in the context of providing professional advice to clients or others.

Practical guidance

This particular mandatory competency is a huge and expansive topic – but it should be kept in perspective. The final assessment panel will keep their testing and questioning within the confines of the knowledge and experience that a person with two years experience in the surveying industry, and occupying a fairly junior position, will have gained. Therefore you will not be expected to have first-hand experience of some of the more detailed areas of the Rules of Conduct, such as your firm's professional indemnity insurance or the Members' Accounts Regulations, but you will be expected to demonstrate your knowledge of the requirements of RICS in these areas and how this would be implemented in practice.

The assessment panel may also test your knowledge around some of the basics, such as why RICS has Rules of Conduct, and aspects of the 12 standards.

Your training should incorporate a mixture of practical experience, structured reading and perhaps some CPD-type events on current issues. This competency is obviously also an ideal subject for your professional development. The APC guidance recommends that training in this area accounts for 16 of the 48 hours per year of professional development experience required.

A useful source of information is the APC guidance on the Rules of Conduct, *RICS guidance note for APC/ATC candidates, supervisors and counsellors: Rules of Conduct*, available from www.rics.org/apc

Levels 2 and 3 will involve you developing your practical experience at work, with an emphasis on taking instructions, understanding and dealing with conflicts of interest, and applying the rules and the 12 standards.

At your three-monthly and six-monthly reviews, you can discuss this with your supervisor and counsellor. You may wish to consider the following:

- *the role and function of RICS*

- *the 12 standards*: How are these applied within your workplace? What examples does your supervisor and counsellor have of situations they have faced?; and

- *Rules of Conduct*: How does your employer ensure that all surveyors comply with these and what policies and procedures are in place?

Some examples of questions asked by assessment panels for this competency are:

- If you are successful with your APC and you decide to start your own business as a chartered surveyor what sort of things will you need to consider and do? For this question, assessors are looking for you to demonstrate that you will:
    - advise RICS that you are starting a business;
    - register for regulation;
    - meet the requirements of the Rules;
    - understand the need for insurances (employers liability, public liability, etc.), a health and safety policy, equal opportunities policy, etc.; and
    - use the RICS logo as set out by RICS and use only the appropriate alternative designation relevant to your professional group.

- What is client's money and how can a firm preserve the security of this? For this question assessors are looking for you to show that you will have systems in place to ensure that clients' money can be clearly linked to the clients to whom it belongs and is protected on their behalf in all circumstances including:
    - insolvency;
    - misappropriation by any party; and
    - death of a sole practitioner.

You should be able to explain that clients' money is any money received and held by a firm that does not solely belong to it. Try to have some examples of clients' money that is relevant to your APC pathway. These might include:

- tenants' deposits;

- rents;

- service charges;

- interest (if in an interest bearing client account);

- arbitration fees;

- fee money taken in advance;

- clients' money held but due to be paid to contractors;

- money held by members appointed as a Receiver; and

- sale proceeds.

You should then explain the systems you would need to have in place including:

- Keeping clients' money in a designated account(s);

- Including the name of the firm and the word 'client' in the name of the account – to distinguish the account from your office account;

- Obtaining bank confirmation of account conditions, including making sure the bank doesn't combine or offset funds in your client account with any other account your firm holds;

- Advising the client on and agree terms of account handling in writing;

- Ensuring there are sufficient funds in the account to pay amounts owing to clients as they fall due under the firm's terms and conditions of engagement;

- Obtaining clients' written approval to make payments from their accounts;

- Banking funds at the earliest reasonable opportunity;
- Nominating authorised staff to handle money;
- Making sure your records show all cash transactions;
- Managing transactions using an accounting system appropriate to the business;
- Using an accounting system that enables you to keep adequate records of your clients' money holdings. A suitable software package will enable the firm to manage money effectively; and
- Reconciling client accounts together with bank and cash balances at regular (usually monthly) intervals in order to demonstrate control over the accuracy and completeness of accounting records.

- If you are successful in undertaking a project for a client and they send you a case of wine as a thank you, what should you do?

  You should clearly state that you would consider whether this could introduce a future conflict of interest. You might also refer to your employer's gift register or other policies/procedures. The important point is to show that you would not accept a gift that may influence your future judgment.

- As a qualified surveyor you are working for a surveying practice and a friend asks you to … [example of work] … as a favour because you are a surveyor, what should you do?

  You should identify that you would not give this advice as you do not have Professional Indemnity Insurance and would encourage your friend to seek advice through your company being careful that you acknowledge any conflict of interest for yourself.

You will see from the above examples how the questions tend to be scenario based and will often take a candidate into areas in which they may not have direct experience.

You should not only be familiar with the RICS Rules of Conduct but also with relevant legislation relating to ethical issues for your pathway and more generally. Of particular general importance is the Bribery Act 2010. This Act replaced the fragmented and complex offences introduced at common law and in the previous Prevention of Corruption Acts. It creates two general offences covering the offering, promising or giving of an advantage, and requesting, agreeing to receive or accepting of an advantage and creates a discrete offence of bribery of a foreign public official. It also creates an offence of failure by a commercial organisation to prevent a bribe being paid for or on its behalf (although it will be a defence if the organisation has adequate procedures in place to prevent bribery). You should ensure you are familiar with this Act and the implications for you as a professional. Guidance can be obtained from the Ministry of Justice website at www.justice.gov.uk.

Testing your ethics knowledge

Ethical standard: Act honourably/Comply with relevant laws and regulations

1. Your client has not yet had the time to ensure that his properties comply with new legislation. He instructs you to act in conflict with legal requirements by using delaying tactics to defer implementation. Your refusal to do so may harm your lucrative business relationship, leading to financial loss. However, to comply with the client's wishes may endanger the lives of his tenants. What should you do?

(a) The client is always right – I would act upon his instruction to maintain our professional relationship.

(b) Ignore the client's wishes – he should have known better than to ask me.

(c) Explain to the client that acting on his instruction would lead to illegal activity. If he still wishes to proceed then advise him that the contract with you will be terminated.

Ethical standard: Be accountable for all your actions

2. You misquoted for a job and find that you significantly underestimated the work involved. Half way through the job you have concerns that you may not satisfactorily be able to carry out the job for this fee. What should you do?

(a) Complete the undertaken job despite incurring a loss and recognising that you must be more careful in future.

(b) Back out of the job.

(c) Try to renegotiate with your client.

Ethical standard: Know and act within your limitations/Be open and transparent in your dealings

3. A client for whom you have worked on many jobs approaches you to undertake a project that will involve you in work in which you have no experience. You don't want to let the client down as they have been an excellent source of fees. What should you do?

(a) Take on the work and read up on the subject.

(b) Advise your client that this is not your area of expertise and recommend another surveyor who you know will do a good job.

(c) Refuse the commission with no explanation as you do not want your client to feel you are not able to do this job.

Ethical standard: Avoid conflicts of interest

4. You are selling land for a client/tendering a contract for a client and obtain an offer/tender bid from a company in which you are a major shareholder. What should you do?

(a)   Sell the land/accept the tender if this is the best bid.

(b)   Advise your client that you are unable to continue with the work.

(c)   Advise all parties of your shareholding interest and your involvement with the client and seek written acceptance to continuing.

5. You are selling land/tendering a contract for a client and one of the developers promises you that if they buy the site/gain the contract they will instruct you to undertake work for them. What should you do?

(a)   Encourage your client to sell/let the contract to this developer.

(b)   Continue the sale/tender making no reference to this approach from the developer.

(c)   Advise your client accordingly and seek their approval to you continuing with the sale/tender.

Ethical standard: Have the courage to make a stand

6. You are aware that properties that you manage/are contract managing the build for do not/will not comply with recently introduced fire safety legislation. New tenants are about to move in. Your client has asked you not to advise them of the discrepancy. What should you do?

(a)   Let your client know that you are not prepared to endanger lives and explain that he must ensure the properties comply with the legislation.

(b)   Accept the client's instruction as you are there to act on his behalf.

(c)   Try to deter the tenants from moving in and encourage them to look for alternative accommodation.

Answers: 1c, 2a, 3b, 4c, 5c, 6a

Finally, you should of course ensure that you provide evidence of this competency in your experience record and professional development record – give examples of structured reading and training and also of practical experience and make sure that all your detailed activities clearly comply with the Rules of Conduct and associated standards.

For further information and guidance on the RICS Rules of Conduct the DVD *RICS Rules of Conduct* available from RICS Books is a very useful resource. The DVD is designed to inform and challenge your knowledge and raise awareness of the depth and the breadth of the Rules of Conduct and what is expected of a professional. The book *Ethics and Professional Conduct for Surveyors* also available from RICS Books is also a useful reference point.

The RICS Regulation website (www.rics.org/ regulation) provides an excellent source of information regarding RICS Rules of Conduct, including details of disciplinary hearings and minutes of the meetings of the Regulatory Board.

> **TOP TIP**
> Always consider the 12 ethical standards.

Client care

This competency is required to be achieved to level 2. At level 1, you should be able to demonstrate a knowledge and understanding of the principle and practice of client care, including:

- the concept of identifying clients, colleagues and third parties who are your clients and understand the behaviours that are appropriate to establish good client relationships;

- the systems and procedures that are appropriate for managing the process of client care including complaints; and

- the requirements to collect data, analyse and define the needs of clients.

At level 2, you should be able to apply all of the above in your area of business or practice on a routine basis.

Practical guidance

Approaches to client care will vary from business to business, depending on the nature of the work, the degree of client interface and the type of organisation. At one extreme – residential valuation, sales and letting – there is a high degree of customer interface, and the skill of managing and influencing clients is vital, with the business relying solely on fee income for survival. In areas of central or local government, by contrast, the link is not so direct and the dependency on fee income from transactions not as great.

However, one key concept is fundamental to all business: the client is sovereign. Notice that this is not the same as saying, 'the customer is always right' – in surveying matters this is not always the case! You must be able to understand the link between customer care and duty of care.

If a client wishes to do something that would be impractical, or impossible, or doomed to certain failure, the surveyor owes the client a duty of care to inform him or her of that. To give the best customer care, you must therefore have a good understanding of each client's needs.

This is one of those competencies where you must be able to 'step back' out of a situation, to analyse what it is that you have learnt about customer care and duty of care in any particular instance. In preparation for the final assessment you should be able to explain a situation in which you have delivered good client care in the context of your work. You should discuss with your supervisor and counsellor opportunities where you can develop skills in this area.

To assist your understanding of this subject, you may also wish to undertake some structured reading and training.

You should familiarise yourself with the RICS requirements regarding Complaints Handling Procedures. Particular points to bear in mind are:

- Whenever terms of engagement are issued, you should make it clear to clients that your firm operates a CHP. However, there is no need to provide your client with a copy at that stage. You should supply the CHP to anyone to whom the firm owes a duty of care who has expressed dissatisfaction with the firm. In certain circumstances it is inappropriate to issue a CHP, for example, where you have been appointed by a court and are legally prohibited from doing so. Where this applies, you should inform your client in writing why you are unable to issue a CHP.

- Complaints should be acknowledged promptly. You should ensure that a full response or (if this is not possible) an update is given within 28 days. Failure to acknowledge or respond and failure to update the client with progress can make the situation worse.

- Complaints should be reviewed by a senior member of a firm or the firm's designated complaints handler. If the complainant remains unhappy with your firm's internal review of the complaint, you should advise that the matter may be referred to your redress scheme. If you are a sole practitioner you may have to review the complaint yourself in the knowledge that, if it cannot be resolved, it must be referred to your approved redress scheme.

- Your firm should keep a log to track complaints received. This will assist your firm in its management of complaints and in making improvements to your procedures based on the complaints pattern identified. Your firm is obliged under the terms of its professional indemnity insurance (PII) policy to tell its insurers about any situation that may give rise to a claim. Issuing your firm's CHP because a client has expressed dissatisfaction or has a query means your firm should inform its insurers as soon as possible to ensure compliance with the terms of your PII policy.

- RICS will become involved only where a firm fails to respond to the complainant or prevents access to an independent redress mechanism.

This competency is very closely related to professional practice and ethics.

You should ensure that you are aware of relevant legislation particularly that relating to discrimination. The Equality Act 2010 is a consolidating Act that covers many of the key areas of discrimination. You should be aware of the fundamental principles of this Act.

TOP TIP

Think about who your clients are. This may be simple if you are in the private sector but if you are in the public or corporate sector, your client may be another department, a board or an individual within your organisation.

Communication and negotiation

This competency is required to be achieved at level 2. At level 1, you are required to demonstrate a knowledge and understanding of effective oral, written, graphic and presentation skills, including methods and techniques appropriate to specific situations. At level 2, you are required to provide evidence of practical application of oral, written, graphic and presentation skills that are appropriate in a variety of situations, specifically where negotiation is involved.

Practical guidance – communication skills

Oral communication is used in a wide range of surveying situations and circumstances: at meetings, in negotiations, when managing people, when making presentations, in tenders, and so on. In my experience, there is some basic best practice for all situations. This can then be tailored to meet the requirements of specific situations. The list of specific situations is of course huge, and training will also be wide and varied.

Communication skills can be improved by additional training. Many organisations run courses in this area – these may include, for example, assertiveness training courses. However, for most candidates, the best approach is to be coached by senior practitioners in your particular area, and to put your developing skills continually into practice.

On a general level, any course or training programme should cover the nature and purposes of oral communication – addressing the different approaches to be taken in different situations, and the techniques that can be used to communicate effectively.

In addition, there are many texts on the subject, allowing training to be complemented by structured reading. A search on the RICS Books website (www.ricsbooks.com) for 'communication skills' will identify a number of excellent publications.

Of course the final assessment interview includes a ten-minute presentation as well as communication via questioning and this, therefore, gives an excellent opportunity for the panel to assess this competency.

Written and graphic communication will cover a wide range of situations and encompass a variety of skills. It will include the use of emails, letters and reports, for all of which an essential component is being able to write good, unambiguous prose.

For level 1, you must be able to understand the various media in which written communications can be presented, and more importantly, the skills involved in doing so, with regard to the target audience, the length, style and layout of the communication, the message you wish to convey, and the structure of the communication. In terms of 'graphic' communication, it covers sketch notes, drawings in plans, designs linked to the construction process and similar (if these are relevant to your chosen pathway).

It is probably easiest to assess understanding with reference to actual written work – your own and other people's – in a variety of mediums. Consider why a particular communication fails or succeeds, how it could be improved, and what the aspects are that make it successful in a particular area.

For level 2, put this knowledge into practice. Consider a range of your written work, in a variety of media. Is it all appropriate for the audience and purpose? Have you achieved, in a letter, report, email, sketch or design what you set out to achieve?

These days there are so many different types of communication medium that it is becoming ever more important to ensure the method you use is appropriate. Methods include:

- letters;
- emails;
- reports;
- telephone;
- meetings;
- telephone conferences;
- web conferences;
- video conferences;
- online social networking;
- blogs;
- text messages; and
- web messaging; to name but a few.

If you are experiencing difficulties in this area, you could attend a course (internal or external) on written communication. There are also a lot of useful books and texts on the subject, again available through RICS Books. Nobody would expect you to write a perfect client report the first time you tried, but with a full understanding of the principles and purposes of the report, and some more practice, you will be much better equipped to do so.

The critical analysis submitted by you for the final assessment provides an easy opportunity for the panel to assess your ability in this area.

Practical guidance – negotiation skills

This competency overlaps somewhat with the 'conflict avoidance' competency (see page 71).

To fulfil the requirements of this particular competency, check that you understand what lies behind successful negotiations: the preparation of evidence; an understanding of the various approaches to negotiations; a knowledge of where and how parameters are set; a knowledge of what each side wishes to get from the negotiations, and from any future relationship; and so on.

If possible, ask your supervisor and counsellor to involve you in negotiations carried out by your firm. This is perhaps the best way of helping you to gain an understanding of the principles and skills.

TOP TIP

Think about who you communicate with and what methods of communication you use and why. Do you always use the most appropriate method of communication?

Health and safety

The basic level 1 requirement of this competency is to demonstrate a knowledge and understanding of the principles and responsibilities with regard to health and safety imposed by law and codes of practice and other regulations relating to health and safety appropriate to your area of practice.

This competency must be taken to level 2 where you will be required to provide evidence of practical application of health and safety issues and the requirements for compliance, in your area of practice.

Practical guidance

This competency covers all aspects of a surveyor's working life. It is about ensuring that the surveyor's entire working life is conducted as safely as possible with as little risk to health as possible, and that the same is true for all of those around the surveyor.

It is easy to think of ways in which health and safety issues relate to, say, work on a construction site, but perhaps less so for more office-based work. However, the same basic philosophies underpin work carried out in any environment. With off-site jobs, the issues encompass such things as your managers knowing where you are and what you are doing at all times, and, should you leave the office, when you will return and who you are meeting. There are also numerous health and safety issues relating to the use of equipment, in offices as well as all other locations, and on keeping employees healthy and safe.

Owing to the importance of health and safety, most firms and organisations conduct formal training and instruction on the relevant issues. Ensure that you attend this and that you can explain the reasons behind any requirements imposed by the firm.

You must be able to demonstrate knowledge of the health and safety legislation and codes of practice that apply to your area of work and the country in which you work. These will differ from one pathway to another. Your evidence should allow you to demonstrate how you have developed this knowledge.

In the UK

Relevant legislation would include the *Health and Safety at Work Act* 1974, the *Construction (Design and Management) Regulations* 2007 and the *Control of Asbestos Regulations* 2006. You should also know and understand the role of the Health and Safety Executive (HSE) which is responsible for health and safety regulation in England and Wales.

HSE owns a significant amount of primary and secondary legislation. The primary legislation comprises the Acts of Parliament, including the *Health and Safety at Work etc Act* 1974. The secondary legislation is made up of Statutory Instruments (SIs), often referred to as regulations. It is enforced by HSE and local authorities (LAs). The HSE and LAs work locally, regionally and nationally to common objectives and standards.

The Health and Safety Executive (HSE) provides numerous free leaflets on its website, at www.hse.gov.uk, including lists of its current publications. You should visit the site and select some useful reading. The website also provides interesting statistics.

The HSE publication *Health and Safety in Great Britain* provides an excellent summary of the legal framework for health and safety in the UK and could be a useful source of structured development for you in this area.

Risk assessment

A risk assessment is a very important element in assessing health and safety risks and you should know and understand how to undertake a risk assessment. I would recommend that you undertake a risk assessment of your own workplace: this could be a useful exercise to be recorded in your experience record (see page 81).

In the UK

The HSE Five Steps to Risk Assessment document is a very useful guide to performing a risk assessment.

Personal safety

Health and safety can also include issues of personal safety and you should consider how you ensure your own safety when out on site, at meetings or travelling for work. Think of ways to ensure your personal safety including:

- Take a fully charged mobile phone with you.

- Carry a highly audible personal alarm.

- Not locking doors behind you.

- Plan your escape route, ideally in two directions.

- Implement a call back system with your office – for example, telephone to say that you are about to start the inspection and that you will phone back at a pre-agreed time to confirm you are safe. Make sure your office knows your phone number as well just in case they need to call you.

- Make your daily work schedule available to others so that they can trace your steps.

- Be very careful about inspecting a roof void and safely position any ladder.

- Park your car close by and ensure you cannot be boxed in. Keep you car keys with you.

- Do not try to move any heavy equipment.

- Make sure the person who greets you is the person you expected to meet. If not, and you are unsure of their status, make an excuse and delay the visit.

- If met by someone under the age of 16, delay the survey until such time as an adult is present.

- If the person you meet appears angry, stay calm and leave if they become abusive or you feel afraid.

- Follow your instinct. If you feel threatened or uncomfortable make an excuse and leave and return with a colleague at another time.

Safety of property

You should always take sensible precautions to protect your personal property, whether you are at home or work.

Electronic gadgets, whether mobile phones, cameras or laptops, are attractive targets for thieves; don't leave them lying around on site or in the office or on view when you leave your car.

You can register any consumer product that has a serial number for free on a website called Immobilise. It's quick and convenient, provides you with a register of property and, in case of loss or theft, can easily be identified and returned to you if found.

Remember:

- Backup your phone numbers and photos in a separate location as a safety precaution.

- Take extra care with clients personal details that maybe stored on electronic equipment.

- Keep all banking details secure, your own and those of clients.

- Use a cross-cut shredder to destroy all personal data if it doesn't need to be kept.

- Keep your personal documents and those of clients, safe from electronic theft.

Personal property of others

As a surveyor you will be visiting properties, homes or sites owned by others and it's important to act with courtesy at all times and to respect other people's property and privacy.

For example:

- Always remove dirty shoes when you enter a property. To make a good impression you could carry some indoor shoes in your equipment bag.

- Take extra care when using tape measures and ladders in confined spaces. It's very easy to knock over an ornament or mark a wall.

- Make sure you leave the space as you found it – put back any items that you move, clear up debris you may have caused and if you damage anything, advise the occupier that your employer will be in contact to arrange suitable compensation.

- Don't use the occupier's personal property without asking, whether it's a broom, a cloth or the downstairs loo!

- Don't read any personal correspondence, private documentation or messages – even if it relates to your task.

- If you see any sexually compromising material, ignore it and resist the urge to make a comment.

- If you feel that there is anything that could be compromise your health or safety make an excuse, leave and discuss it with your employer.

TOP TIP
Remember health and safety can be just that but also can be personal safety, safety of your personal property and the safety of property of others.

TOP TIP
If you visit construction sites or are likely to, consider gaining your Construction Skills Certification Scheme Card. You will need this when out on site and it can also be used as evidence towards this competency.

Accounting principles and procedures

This competency must be achieved to level 1. The requirement is to demonstrate knowledge and understanding of fundamental accounting concepts plus the format and preparation of management and company accounts, including profit and loss statements, cash flow statements and balance sheets.

Practical guidance

You will undoubtedly be able to gain some experience – practical or theoretical – of these concepts in the course of your work. If there is one particular aspect that is unlikely to arise in your everyday work, consider how your training might be arranged so that this is covered.

You may also like to read a textbook on the subject, or attend an appropriate training course or CPD lecture.

It should be noted that some candidates might quite easily reach levels 2 and 3 in this competency, if this subject is part of your job. For example, a rural practice candidate working for an estate would deal with these types of issues regularly. Candidates working in commercial property and dealing, perhaps, with the leisure and entertainments industry, might also easily attain level 2 or 3 through practical experience, particularly where accounts are used for valuation purposes.

If you are not able to gain direct experience for this competency in your job, then consider arranging to spend some time with an accountant either within your company or outside.

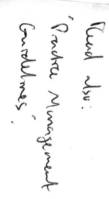

anning

.cy must be achieved to level 1. The
to demonstrate knowledge and
; of how business management activities
the achievement of corporate objectives.

ance

t subject, and most candidates generally
tending some kind of basic management
trai..... urse, where possible. These are run by a
number of bodies, including Open University and the
Chartered Management Institute. Many employers also
offer training in this area. You may well not be directly
involved in managing your business, and this is not
expected of you for the purposes of level 1, but you must
be able to understand – and explain to the assessors, if
necessary – the underlying factors of business
management.

A lot will also be learned on the job, of course, and
coaching and training from an experienced supervisor or
counsellor will be invaluable. There is a lot of overlap
with the requirements of the other mandatory
competencies (communications and negotiation,
teamworking, client care, and so on). Reading a
management skills textbook will also develop knowledge
and understanding of issues such as motivation, mission
statements, strategy, organisational structures, and so on.

A useful textbook in this respect is *The handbook of
management and leadership: a guide to managing for
results* by Michael Armstrong and Tina Stephens (Kogan
Page, London, 2005). This book covers the practice of
management, delivering change, enhancing customer
relations and enabling continuous improvement.

Conflict avoidance, management and dispute resolution procedures

This competency must be achieved to level 1. This requires knowledge and understanding of the techniques for conflict avoidance, conflict management and dispute resolution procedures, including for example adjudication and arbitration appropriate to your APC pathway.

Practical guidance

The 'ingredients' of this competency will vary greatly between the various pathways. In commercial practice, for example, landlord and tenant matters will be fairly common, while in construction, this competency will be present everyday in managing building contracts. Indeed, in the construction pathway (Quantity surveying and Construction), this becomes a core competency to level 2, with requirements based around procurement and the drafting of terms and conditions of leases, contracts and agreements.

In basic terms, and across all pathways, it is important that you understand how to conduct negotiations, and also the various options available should negotiations break down, working through mediation and conciliation, adjudication, arbitration, independent expert determination, and, finally, litigation.

You may be encouraged to sit in on negotiations at your firm from an early stage in your career. Also you will benefit from some formal training on this and other aspects of dispute resolution, covering the preparation of evidence, case law, approaches and tactics. It is reasonably likely that by the time you reach the final assessment, you will have had practical experience of running your own negotiations, or participating in other dispute resolution procedures, and will thus be able to discuss this. As part of your training plan ensure that you make steady progress towards this end.

There are also many texts available on this subject. To get started, the following RICS guidance notes and practice statements are useful documents:

- *Surveyors acting as arbitrators and as independent experts in commercial property rent reviews*;

- *Surveyors acting as adjudicators in the construction industry*;

- *Surveyors acting as expert witnesses*; and

- *Surveyors acting as advocates.*

All of these publications are available in hardcopy from RICS Books (www.ricsbooks.com). RICS members can download the publications as a PDF from www.rics.org

Specific issues to be aware of are:

Mediation

Mediation is the name given to a confidential process whereby parties to a dispute invite a neutral individual to facilitate negotiations between them with a view to achieving a resolution of their dispute.

Arbitration

An arbitration is a legal proceeding under the Arbitration Acts and the arbitrator reaches a decision on the basis of evidence put before them sometimes at a formal hearing. The arbitrator can call for discovery of documents and interprets the evidence. The arbitrator's decision is enforceable as if it were a judgment of the court. Although the arbitrator is not liable for negligence the court can set the judgment aside on the grounds of misconduct.

Independent expert

An independent expert is appointed jointly by the two parties to give an expert opinion on the matter to be decided. The expert may have regard to evidence submitted or may have a hearing and adopt what they consider to be the most appropriate procedure. The expert's decision is not enforceable directly by the courts and they are liable for action for negligence.

The RICS Disputes Resolution Professional Group website provides some really good guidance in this area. See www.rics.org/drs

For this competency you should also ensure that you are aware of the RICS requirements regarding complaints handling.

In addition, don't forget CPD-type lectures or training that may be available within your firm, or from external providers.

Data management

This competency must be achieved to level 1. It involves demonstrating knowledge and understanding of the sources of information and data applicable to your area of practice, including the methodologies and techniques most appropriate to collect, collate and store data.

Practical guidance

Again, this competency will vary greatly between the APC pathways. It is important to think of it in relation to your specific route, and against the backdrop of your day-to-day work and the particular IT developments in your area.

In the valuation pathway, for example, this competency will cover comparable evidence found in sales and rental evidence. Collection, collation and storage methods in this pathway will usually comprise the use of IT spreadsheets and databases, either developed by firms or sold as commercial packages. Developments in this area, and in the commercial property pathway, include the use of computer assisted techniques.

In the quantity surveying and construction pathway, meanwhile, sources of data may be previous contracts or cost guides and price books. Various commercial packages are also available to price contracts and bills of quantities.

For all pathways, the important thing is for you to be able to understand the use of data in your day-to-day work – how this is gathered and put to use, and what the best methods of collection, collation and storage are. You should be able to step back mentally from your work, to explain what data you use, how you find it and how it is manipulated. You should also be aware of the implications of data protection legislation and how this will affect the use that can be made of data you may hold.

You should avoid the temptation to 'write this competency off', on the basis that it will be covered at level 1 elsewhere – for example, in level 1 of the valuation competency. Try to use the competency to broaden and develop your understanding of wider data issues and developments in the profession. See this competency as a subject in itself and carry out some structured reading. Discuss it as a discrete issue at some point in your training plan and at the three- and six-monthly assessment stages.

Within your work you will use many different sources of information, including:

- colleagues;
- documents;

- the internet;
- data;
- books;
- journals;
- companies;
- government departments;
- files; and many more.

It is worthwhile thinking over your recent work and considering what information you have used and from where it came. Think also of other information that your organisation may have provided to others. Who needed this and why?

When you have information you need to consider what you are able to do with it. This may not be as straightforward as you might think because of laws that deal with the handling of information.

In the UK

You need to familiarise yourself with the following legislation.

The ***Data Protection Act* 1998** gives individuals the right to know what information is held about them. It provides a framework to ensure that personal information is handled properly.

The Act works in two ways. Firstly, it states that anyone who processes personal information must comply with eight principles, which make sure that personal information is:

- fairly and lawfully processed;
- processed for limited purposes;
- adequate, relevant and not excessive;

- accurate and up to date;
- not kept for longer than is necessary;
- processed in line with your rights;
- secure; and
- not transferred to other countries without adequate protection.

The second area covered by the Act provides individuals with important rights, including the right to find out what personal information is held on computer and most paper records.

Should an individual or organisation feel they are being denied access to personal information that they are entitled to, or feel their information has not been handled according to the eight principles, they can contact the Information Commissioner's Office (ICO) for help. Complaints are usually dealt with informally, but if this is not possible, enforcement action can be taken.

The *Data Protection Act* does not guarantee personal privacy at all costs, but aims to strike a balance between the rights of individuals and the sometimes competing interests of those with legitimate reasons for using personal information. It applies to some paper records as well as computer records.

This short checklist will help you understand how to comply with the *Data Protection Act*. Being able to answer 'yes' to every question does not guarantee compliance, and you may need more advice in particular areas, but it should mean that you are heading in the right direction.

- Do I really need this information about an individual? Do I know what I'm going to use it for?
- Do the people whose information I hold know that I've got it, and are they likely to understand what it will be used for?

- If I'm asked to pass on personal information, would the people about whom I hold information expect me to do this?

- Am I satisfied the information is being held securely, whether it's on paper or on computer? And what about my website? Is it secure?

- Is access to personal information limited to those with a strict need to know?

- Am I sure the personal information is accurate and up to date?

- Do I delete or destroy personal information as soon as I have no more need for it?

- Do I need to arrange for the Information Commissioner to be notified?

The *Freedom of Information Act* 2000 deals with access to official information, while other regulations deal with environmental information.

The Act provides individuals or organisations with the right to request information held by a public authority. Information must also be published through the public authority's publication scheme. This must be approved by the ICO, and is a commitment by a public authority to make certain information available, and a guide on how to obtain it.

The Act applies to all information, not just information filed since the Act came into force.

In Scotland the relevant legislation is the *Freedom of Information (Scotland) Act* 2002.

Sustainability

As a mandatory competency this is required to level 1. It requires a knowledge and understanding of why and how sustainability seeks to balance economic, environmental and social objectives at local, national and global levels, in the context of land, property and the built environment.

Practical guidance

All chartered surveyors need a basic understanding of environmental issues, which range from groundwater pollution and contaminated land, to control of pollution in the air we breathe, as well as, very importantly, energy and climate change. Environmental issues affect building design, construction use and management, development and redevelopment, and regeneration and town planning. Issues such as global warming, dwindling national resources and atmospheric pollutants are top priorities with many government and influential bodies, such as the EU and the World Trade Organisation (WTO).

You should carry out some general reading in newspapers and professional journals on environmental issues. Other useful sources of information and advice are the RICS guidance notes:

- *Contamination and environmental issues – their implications for property professionals*;

- *Sustainability and the RICS property lifecycle*; and

- *Carbon management of real estate*.

Surveying Sustainability: a short guide for the property professional, produced in partnership between RICS, Forum for the Future and Gleeds is also useful.

In addition, of course, you should maintain an awareness of environmental issues while at work. You should be aware of any government initiatives, laws or EU regulations affecting your particular area of work. The Department of Energy and Climate Change (DECC) website is a useful resource (www.decc.gov.uk). On a more local level, be aware of any internal office environmental policies (recycling of paper, for example), and be able to explain the purposes of these. You may like to test your knowledge and understanding in this area by considering how you would express the firm's 'green credentials', should this be requested, for example, in an invitation to tender. Once more, this is a case of stepping back from day-to-day work, to consider the environmental factors that underlie and overarch such work.

> **TOP TIP**
> Policy and legislation regarding sustainability are constantly evolving. You should ensure you keep up to date by reading daily newspapers or news sites regularly and property or construction journals.

Teamworking

This competency is required to level 1. Candidates must demonstrate knowledge and understanding of the principles, behaviour and dynamics of teamworking.

Practical guidance

This competency involves understanding why people work in teams, and some of the basic principles underlying teamworking. In practice, you will rarely not work within a team, so in effect, while the mandatory requirement is to level 1, in practice you will often be working to level 2 ('working as a team member in a work or business environment').

Evidence of working in a team will be easy to come by; however, the level 1 requirement is to *understand the principles* behind this. You should therefore consider a situation in which you have witnessed or experienced teamworking, and be able to explain how that team worked, concentrating on the roles each member adopted and the success, or otherwise, of this.

Your understanding can be complemented and extended by some reading on the subject. A leading text on this subject is *Management teams: Why they succeed or fail* by R. M. Belbin (Butterworth-Heinemann, Oxford, 2003).

Background

In the past thirty years or so, teamworking has grown in importance. Until relatively recently, roles at work were well-defined. In the traditional manufacturing industry, for example, there was strict division of responsibilities and most job titles conveyed exactly what people did. However, with advances in technology and education, employers began to place a growing emphasis on versatility, leading to an increasing interest in teamworking at all levels. The gradual replacement of traditional hierarchical forms with flatter organisational structures, in which employees are expected to fill a variety of roles, has also played a part in the rise of the team.

You should consider the following issues:

- What is a team?

- Types of team

- Benefits of teamworking

Stages of team development

The main stages of team development are generally considered to be as follows:

- Forming (or undeveloped) – when people are working as individuals rather than a team.

- Storming – teams need to pass through a stage of conflict if they are to achieve their potential. The team becomes more aggressive, both internally and in relation to outside groups, rules and requirements.

- Norming (or consolidating) – the team is beginning to achieve its potential, effectively applying the resource it has to the tasks it has, using a process it has developed itself.

- Performing – when the team is characterised by openness and flexibility. It challenges itself constantly but without emotionally charged conflict, and places a high priority on the development of other team members.

- Mourning – when the team disbands.

While this is a useful theoretical model, it should not be seen as unvarying. For example, a mature performing team may revert to an earlier stage if something happens, perhaps the loss of a key member or a threatening change in the organisation. Alternatively, a team in which the members know each other well may perform almost from the start.

Characteristics of effective teams

An effective team has the following characteristics:

- a common sense of purpose;

- a clear understanding of the team's objectives;

- resources to achieve those objectives;

- mutual respect among team members, both as individuals and for the contribution each makes to the team's performance;

- a valuing of members' strengths and respecting their weaknesses;

- mutual trust;

- a willingness to share knowledge and expertise;

- a willingness to speak openly;

- a range of skills among team members to deal effectively with all its tasks;

- a range of personal styles for the various roles needed to carry out the team's tasks.

Team role theories and team selection

There are two requirements in selecting team members: the team should include a range of the necessary technical and specialist skills, and there should be a variety of personal styles among members to fill the different roles that are involved in successful teamwork. The pioneering work on team roles or types was carried out by Dr Meredith Belbin in the 1970s. He lists nine team roles:

- Plant – creative, imaginative, unorthodox; solves difficult problems.

- Resource investigator – extrovert, enthusiastic, exploratory; explores opportunities; develops contacts.

- Coordinator – mature, confident, a good chairperson; clarifies goals; promotes decision making.

- Shaper – dynamic, challenging; has drive and courage to overcome obstacles.

- Monitor evaluator – sober, strategic, discerning; sees all options.

- Teamworker – cooperative, mild, perceptive, diplomatic; listens, builds, averts friction.

- Implementer – disciplined, reliable, conservative; turns ideas into practical action.

- Completer – painstaking, conscientious, anxious; searches out errors and omissions, delivers on time.

- Specialist – single-minded, self-starting, dedicated; provides knowledge and skill in rare supply.

Team size

Most commentators suggest that between five and eight people is the ideal size for teams. Teams need to be large enough to incorporate the appropriate range of expertise and representation of interests, but not so large that people's participation, and hence their interest, is limited.

And finally on teamworking

Teams come in many forms and exist for many purposes. Teamworking is desirable in many circumstances and, properly managed, can contribute to improved organisational performance, while improving individuals' job satisfaction and helping to empower them. But not all teams succeed. Inadequate terms of reference, poor selection of team members, inadequate resources, the wrong mix of personality types and skills, the wrong size, inadequate training and poor leadership are among the reasons why teams fail.

> **TOP TIP**
> While there are academic theories of teamworking some of which I have described here, you should consider the teams you work in and with. What do you think make these successful?

A last word of advice

Hopefully you now have a better idea of what the mandatory competencies entail, and of how to achieve them. Remember that the philosophies behind the mandatory competencies, and the business skills inherent in them, will be encountered in every aspect of your working life. It is for this reason that they are mandatory!

The guidance here only deals with the competencies in relation to the training period. We will return to the competencies when we look at the final assessment interview in chapter 5; for now, simply note that the final assessment interview is a largely competency-based interview, although some questions may relate to matters of a more general nature.

Professional development

For each 12 months of practical training that is completed, you must undertake an annual minimum of 48 hours of professional development. If you are studying for your RICS accredited degree by part time study or distance learning while undertaking your APC structured training period then the final year of your study can be used towards your professional development for that year. You should however undertake additional professional development to supplement this.

The idea behind professional development is that it gives you the opportunity to acquire some of the additional skills and knowledge that it will not always be possible for your employer to provide within the week-to-week business of the practice. The APC guidance recommends that you undertake 16 hours per year of professional development in:

- personal skills development linked to mandatory competencies;

- technical skills development linked to your core and optional competencies; and

- professional practice skills development linked to professional practice competencies, code of conduct and conflicts of interest.

When you record your professional development activity in your professional development record you will be asked to allocate each activity to one of the above categories.

The professional development record template is shown in figure 2, with example entries.

RICS

Candidate Name - 1234567
Template 4
Graduate Route 1

Professional Development Record

Commercial property practice

Please detail the PD / LLL development title, location and key components. Include Method of Learning. Include an overview of the objective and reasoning why you are doing this PD / LLL development. Conclude with the outcome and how it relates to your declared competencies.

Year 1			
Date	Subject (objective, reasoning and outcome)	Hours	PD Split?
01/02/2010	RICS Red Book seminar. Attended to gain a better understanding of the Red Book. I now know and understand the status of the Red Book, the valuations to which it applies and the relevant requirements.	3.0	Technical
10/03/2010	CRC Energy Efficiency Scheme. Internet research using the DECC website to gain an understanding of the scheme. I now understand the businesses to which this applies and how we might better advise our clients as to how they may meet the requirements of the Scheme.	2.0	Technical
15/03/2010	Rent review case law. Undertook structured use of EGi to research rent review case law over the last 12 months. I now have a good understanding of case precedents that may impact on rent reviews I may deal with in the course of my work.	5.0	Technical
19/03/2010	RICS Rules of Conduct for Members. Structured reading of the RICS Rules of Conduct and associated helpsheets to ensure I am familiar with these Rules. I now know the 12 standards that underpin the Rules and have a good understanding of what I need to do in order to comply.	3.0	Professional
23/03/2010	In-house negotiation training. To help to develop my negotiation skills for my rent review and lease renewal work. I have learnt new techniques that will help me to negotiate the best outcome for my client.	3.0	Personal
dd/mm/yyyy		0.0	Select a Split
dd/mm/yyyy		0.0	Select a Split
dd/mm/yyyy		0.0	Select a Split
dd/mm/yyyy		0.0	Select a Split
dd/mm/yyyy		0.0	Select a Split
dd/mm/yyyy		0.0	Select a Split
dd/mm/yyyy		0.0	Select a Split
dd/mm/yyyy		0.0	Select a Split
dd/mm/yyyy		0.0	Select a Split
dd/mm/yyyy		0.0	Select a Split
dd/mm/yyyy		0.0	Select a Split
dd/mm/yyyy		0.0	Select a Split
		16.0	Total

Note: 96 hours in total required for Final Assessment (minimum 48 hours per year)

Hours	Total / Split
3.0	Personal
10.0	Technical
3.0	Professional

Figure 2 Professional development record

An important aspect of your professional development is that it should be planned and structured in such a way that it remains flexible. It should be designed to complement and support your training and development in the context of the various competencies. Professional development may comprise formal training courses or more informal types of learning, such as structured reading, distance-learning or e-learning programmes and secondments. It is important that you accept ownership of your professional development, recognising that the planning, acquiring and evaluating of it is your responsibility. Note that the APC guidance also provides excellent advice on professional development and in particular the principles which underpin professional development, such as it should:

- be gained in a structured manner;

- be based on an explicit process of selecting, planning and evaluating the activities; and

- reflect learning from informal training sources such as structured reading and secondments.

On a practical note, make sure that your professional development complements your structured training agreement, and ensure that you can provide evidence of a planned and systematic approach. There should be a clearly defined relationship between the topics selected and the competencies. If you feel that there is a need for variation regarding the number of hours allocated, discuss this with your supervisor and counsellor.

Structured training

In the context of the APC, this is training that is discussed, planned, reviewed and, if necessary, revised, and which, most importantly, forms the basis of an agreement between the parties.

The development of a structured training agreement is mandatory for all candidates and is prepared by your employer. It must be approved by your RICS training advisor and once approved your employer will be listed as holding an RICS approved structured training agreement on the RICS website.

Structured training agreement

The purpose and status of a structured training agreement (STA) is:

- To identify the breadth and depth of relevant experience needed to fulfil the APC competencies, and plan your work to achieve this. A separate structured training programme (STP) will be devised for each candidate working for your employer, but this does not have to be separately approved by RICS.

- To be an agreement between the employer and RICS, stating the intended policy for implementing RICS' requirements and administration of the APC training process. It is up to your employer to update the STA in light of changes to work practices, or changes to the RICS procedures and requirements.

- A statement of how your employer intends to implement the requirements of the APC process. It also tells you what you can expect from your employer, and what your employer expects from you, based on the official APC guidance. It is a declaration of intent, and statement of expectation.

- An agreement from your employer to comply with the APC training process as detailed in the official APC guidance and in accordance with the RICS Rules of Conduct.

- To guide your employer in producing a specific STP for each candidate, preferably, prior to registration and to confirm that your employer has the will, means and intention of supporting all APC candidates through to final assessment. You and your employer should then use the STP as a management tool to ensure that you get to final interview as soon as possible.

- A requirement that once the STA and STP has been approved, it is your employer's responsibility to ensure that it is implemented effectively and completely.

There is a template available for download from www.rics.org/apc for use by your employer when developing a structured training agreement and a structured training programme.

Your employer should submit the STA to RICS for approval. You should not submit this for approval yourself. It need only be approved once, per employer, although different STAs may be needed for different APC pathways.

The STP should be signed by yourself and your counsellor after approval of the STA has been given by RICS.

RICS APC guides and Pathway guides must be used in conjunction with the STA. This document does not replace them.

If your employer needs any advice regarding the updating of the approved STA or STP or has queries on implementing the APC procedures, you should encourage them to contact RICS.

You will find that most employers who have recently trained APC candidates will already have an approved training agreement in place and will be familiar with RICS requirements.

If a structured training agreement is not in place or a new agreement is needed, the guidance at www.rics.org/apc will provide a useful discussion document for you and your employer when planning and agreeing your training. Your employer may also invite an RICS training adviser to come in to talk through the requirements for structured training.

The structured training agreement template provides guidance only – your employer may wish to tailor an agreement more suited to his or her firm. The following information should generally be included within a structured training agreement:

- statements of commitment by your employer;

- information on the organisation and areas of activity;

- information on the organisation's policies regarding training and the APC, including how the professional development requirement will be met and supported; and

- a commitment to preparing a training programme for each candidate, including arrangements and timescales for monitoring the training programme.

Your training programme should comprise:

- a competency achievement planner setting out your chosen competencies and the timescales within which your supervisor and counsellor hope you will achieve each level of each competency; and

- details of the experience that will be available for each level of each competency that you need to achieve.

TOP TIP

Ask your employer to contact your local RICS training adviser for advice regarding the development of a structured training agreement. RICS must approve the plan.

Summary

- Competencies are written to three levels and are generally progressive in terms of skills and abilities.

- There is no minimum requirement for the number of days needed to achieve each competency. The level of attainment is decided by you, your supervisor and your counsellor together.

- Mandatory competencies are compulsory for all candidates.

- Professional development should be linked to and used to complement your experience and linked to your competencies. At the final assessment your documentation must show evidence of a planned and systematic approach to professional development.

- Structured training is training that is discussed, planned and reviewed between the parties to the agreement. RICS training advisers (RTAs) can provide your employer with advice and support to help with developing a structured training agreement.

- An organisation's overall structured training agreement must be approved by RICS (this is not required for each and every candidate once an approval has been given).

Information management

3

This chapter looks at the various records that you need to keep during the training period. It provides advice and guidance on how to keep these records and considers their importance in the context of the final assessment. The role of the supervisor and counsellor is also covered.

Why keep records?

You should be aware of the importance of the various records you need to keep in the context of both your continuous training and the final assessment. The information contained in your candidate achievement record, professional development record and experience record will not only provide the assessment panel with the evidence that you have met the minimum training requirements, but will also give a focus for lines of questioning during the final assessment interview. It is therefore vital that you manage and record this information during the training period in an organised and systematic manner, as this will greatly assist you in the final interview.

The records

Most of the records you need to keep have been considered briefly in outline in the previous chapters. The following guidance brings all of this together and provides some practical tips and advice.

Diary

A diary must be kept by all candidates. This is simply a
day-to-day record of your training and experience.

Date	Nature of professional work carried out	Competency reference
01/03/10	**Commercial property/valuation pathway**	
	Phoned local agents and researched our company database to obtain comparables for valuation of 1 High Street, Old Town for sale purposes (1/2 day).	T083
	Inspected 2 Low Street, New Town in order to prepare sales particulars (1/2 day).	T044
01/03/10	**Building surveying pathway**	
	Prepared survey report for potential purchaser of Unit 1, New Town Industrial Park prior to acquisition of unit (1/2 day).	T006
	Undertook inspection prior to preparation of Energy Performance Certificate for Unit 3, Old Park.	T044
01/03/10	**Quantity surveying and construction pathway**	
	Reviewed submitted tender docs for 1 Retail Park, Old Town.	T062
	Site visit to Morrisons supermarket site, Old Town to discuss delays due to weather conditions.	T017

Figure 3 Diary template with example entries

The diary will provide the information and detail that
you will need to summarise in your experience record. It
is also a very useful document to use to remind your
supervisor and your counsellor of the detail of the work
with which you have been involved between each of their
assessments.

Your diary is not submitted as part of the final
assessment documentation. However, it should always be
kept up to date and be available for inspection by your
RICS training adviser (RTA) on an office visit or by the

final assessment panel, if requested. You can start recording experience after you have received confirmation of your enrolment (RICS will allow you to back date your experience for up to a month provided you have been employed by your current employer for that time – contact the Membership Operations department for more detail). The date shown in the acknowledgment of enrolment from RICS should, therefore, be the first entry in your diary. Remember that if you change employer, this must be clearly marked, with perhaps a couple of parallel lines to show a break and a few words of explanation. You must also advise RICS of this change by completing and returning the change of employer form available from www.rics.org/apc

There are five important pieces of advice regarding your diary:

1 Keep it up to date. Get into the habit of writing up your experience on a weekly basis.

2 Only record experience in the core and optional competency areas, not the mandatory.

3 Record your experience in periods of no less than half a day (this may involve some 'packaging' of experience that has taken place over the week – so long as the balance of experience over the week in total is accurate, this is fine).

4 Get into the habit of using descriptions that relate to the various competencies, so that you can make easy links to your experience and candidate achievement records and to the competency achievement planner in your structured training agreement. For example, 'negotiation and agreement of repair works under a final schedule of dilapidations' will give you all of the links and reminders you need to properly complete your other documentation. It will also help when

your supervisor and counsellor are reviewing your overall performance against your competency achievement planner.

5   You should use your diary as part of the preparation process for the final assessment. It is therefore important that it is well written and clearly presented, to help you when you are reviewing your training and experience over the two-year period (if you are a graduate route 1 candidate), in preparation for the final assessment interview.

Candidate achievement record

The candidate achievement record includes your log book and your log book summary.

Your log book is a summary of the number of days of work experience recorded in your diary, for each competency, for each month of the training period.

	Candidate Name - 1234567												
Log Book - Year 1	**Commercial Property**												**Template 3**
	Months												
Number and Competency Title	1	2	3	4	5	6	7	8	9	10	11	12	Total
	Month	Month	Month	Month	Month	Month	Month	Month	Month	Month	Month	Month	Days
	Year	Year	Year	Year	Year	Year	Year	Year	Year	Year	Year	Year	
Technical - Core Competencies													
Technical - Optional Competencies													
Technical - Plus Competencies													
	Total												

Figure 4 Format for the log book

Get into the discipline of completing your log book at the end of each month. The log book is a very useful tool for the assessment panel. It provides an immediate snapshot of your areas of work experience and will be used, in conjunction with your experience record, to structure the final assessment interview to reflect your experience and your competency achievements.

You should complete your log book summary after each of your supervisor's and counsellor's assessments to reflect the competency achievements that have been confirmed by your supervisor or your counsellor at that time.

Professional development

Be proactive in recording your professional development. As explained in chapter 2, there are many aspects of your daily work that count as professional development, such as attending meetings, preparing to run a meeting or give a talk, structured reading, and so on. Make sure that you are fully aware of what constitutes professional development, and for further information take a look at www.rics.org/apc. Keep a regular record in your personal diary – this record can then be transferred on a monthly basis to your professional development record. Do make sure that when you record time for professional development you do not also allocate this time as work experience. It can only be one or the other!

Experience record

The experience record is a record of your experience and training against your competencies. You should complete this record before each of your supervisor and counsellor assessments, using the document to summarise your diary for each of the competencies where you have gained further experience in that period. In total, for each level, once achieved you should aim to have written up to 200 words. You should give a summary of your diary experience and supplement this with some specific examples of work with which you have been involved. You should ideally name these real life projects but if confidentiality is an issue then you should simply explain the type of project. The pathway guides will be very useful in helping to steer you towards the types of experience to consider, including for each level of each competency. After all, this is what the assessors will use to steer their questions for the final assessment. Unlike the diary, you do need to discuss the mandatory competencies in your experience record so it may be useful to keep a separate note of experience in these areas to inform your experience record. Figure 5 shows a section of the experience record template for the commercial property pathway.

You should aim to make the experience record the focal point of your meetings with your supervisor at three-monthly intervals and with your counsellor at six-monthly intervals. You need to be proactive in managing your progress. Therefore, prepare this record in advance of these meetings, in order that it can be used by your supervisor and counsellor in assessing your progress.

Progress reports

The role of your supervisor and counsellor throughout the training period is most important. Detailed guidance on these roles and responsibilities is available at www.rics.org/apc. There are, however, a few key issues worth noting:

- The supervisor is responsible for overseeing your day-to-day work, whereas the counsellor is responsible for managing your training at a strategic level;

- ideally, the supervisor and counsellor should be different people. However, the roles may be combined if, for instance, you are employed by a sole practitioner or if there are other reasons why it is appropriate that one person covers the two roles;

	Candidate Name - 1234567
	Template 6
	Graduate Route 1

Experience Record

Commercial property practice

Please record your summary of experience / training completed against your declared competencies. **Note: Record against ALL declared Levels up to a maximum of 1000 characters per cell (approximately 150 to 200 words per Level).** (PD / LLL should be recorded in Template 4).

Competency & level	Competency experience details	Job title / Employer
Technical - Core Competencies		
T044 Inspection		
T044 Inspection Level 1		
T044 Inspection Level 2		
T044 Inspection Level 3		
T057 Measurement of land and property		
T057 Measurement of land and property Level 1		
T057 Measurement of land and property Level 2		
T057 Measurement of land and property Level 3		
T083 Valuation		
T083 Valuation Level 1	I have attended two valuation updates which have helped to develop my knowledge of the five methods of valuation. I have also undertaken valuations for sale purposes where I have used the investment and profits method and for asset valuation purposes for a local authority where I have used the DRC. I have read the Red Book and refer to this when undertaking valuations. I have undertaken a number of valuations of properties where I have needed to take account of planning, building regulations and sustainability issues.	AB Surveyors Ltd
T083 Valuation Level 2	I have prepared terms of engagement for valuation instructions for a range of different purposes including loan security and asset valuation. I have also undertaken a wide range of valuations for sale, purchase, rent review, loan security and accounts purposes. This has involved undertaking the inspection both of the property and a review of the local area, obtaining comparables from our firm's database and from other agents in the area and preparing the valuation itself. I have also drafted valuation reports in accordance with the Red Book for consideration and sign off by my supervisor. I have undertaken valuations in both strong and weak market conditions. I have recently been involved in a valuation of a shop in a high street where there have been very few lettings or sales in the last two years. This involved adjusting comparables to reflect the changes in market conditions. I have also recently been involved in a valuation of a restaurant where I needed to take full account of the strength of the current occupier in adjusting my analysis of the trade.	CD Surveyors Ltd
T083 Valuation Level 3	I have undertaken valuations using a range of different techniques depending upon my client's requirements and the requirements of the instruction. These have included desk top valuations and full Red Book valuation reports. The types of properties I have valued have had a range of different attributes, some have had physical defects that I have needed to account for, some have had development potential and some have had very low environmental credentials. This work has involved me in making adjustments in my valuations to reflect these issues. I have undertaken valuations for rent reviews, lease renewals, assignments, purchase, sale, asset valuations and loan security. I have undertaken valuations of both leasehold and freehold interests. This has included valuations of long leasehold leases and ground leases as well as short (3 to 5 year) lease terms. I have also used the comparable method to value some residential properties.	CD Surveyors Ltd

Figure 5 Experience record template with example entries

- Both parties should be chartered surveyors. In some cases the supervisor does not need to be a chartered surveyor but the counsellor must;

- The supervisor should give guidance, support and encouragement on a regular basis and will usually be your line manager. At three-monthly intervals, they will assess your progress against the competencies and complete your progress reports;

- The counsellor has a similar but more strategic role, and will formally assess your progress on a six-monthly basis and complete the appropriate progress report. In reviewing your overall progress, the counsellor will provide a second opinion to that of the supervisor. The counsellor will also consider any adjustments that may be needed to your training in order for you to meet the necessary competencies.

- Your supervisor and counsellor have responsibility with regard to confirming on your final assessment submission that your documentation is a true and accurate representation of your training and experience.

You must take a positive approach to the meetings during the training period to discuss progress. Make sure that you agree the times and dates for these meetings and are prepared to give your input. As explained previously, use the experience record as the focal point for these meetings. Remember that your final assessment will be based on your performance and competency statements and levels, and it is therefore important that your training and experience are geared towards this. The regular meetings with your supervisor and counsellor will be the ideal opportunity to review progress and to plan how you will fill any gaps.

Templates are available from www.rics.org/apc for progress reports to be prepared by your supervisor and your counsellor. These are not submitted to RICS but are a useful tool for recording the discussions at your assessments and your supervisor's and counsellor's views of your progress.

TOP TIP

Use your experience record as the focal point for your assessments with your supervisor and counsellor and make sure this is prepared for them well in advance of these assessment meetings.

Summary

- The information and evidence contained in your diary, candidate achievement record, professional development record and experience record are very important. They will be used both by your supervisor and counsellor in their assessments and in the final assessment to satisfy the panel that you meet the training and experience requirements of the APC.

- Your diary must be available for inspection if requested by an RTA or the assessment panel.

- Get into the habit of completing your diary weekly, your log book monthly and your experience record and log book summary at least quarterly.

- The candidate achievement record comprises the log book and the log book summary. The log book provides details of the numbers of days experience you have had in each competency each month and the log book summary provides the number of days each year for each competency and the competency levels that have been achieved as assessed by your supervisor and your counsellor.

- Be proactive in all meetings with your supervisor and counsellor. Plan and prepare for them.

Preparation for the final assessment

4

This chapter covers the months in the run-up to the final assessment interview. It considers the paperwork that needs to be completed for the final assessment. In order to assist your preparation, it provides detailed guidance on the methodology that will be adopted by the panel during the interview. Finally, advice on preparing the final assessment record and the critical analysis is given.

The paperwork

You will have decided your target final assessment date with your supervisor and your counsellor at the beginning of your APC journey. The earliest date you can apply for final assessment is after you have recorded at least 22 months of experience for graduate route 1 or 10 months of experience for graduate route 2, satisfied the minimum competency levels for your pathway and undertaken the required number of hours of professional development and days of recorded experience.

To apply for final assessment: send your final assessment application form to RICS during the dates shown on www.rics.org. You will then have one month to complete and send to RICS your final assessment submissions. At the final assessment as a graduate route 1 candidate you must have recorded at least 23 months of experience and if you are a graduate route 2 candidate then you must have recorded at least 11 months of experience. These submissions must be complete or you will not be eligible to take the final assessment. Once these submissions are received by RICS, you will be sent a confirmation letter with the date, time and venue of your final assessment. You will be sent these details around one month prior to your assessment. There are two important points to note with regard to this:

1   If you do not wish to sit your final assessment on the proposed date, the onus is on you to notify RICS that you are deferring and this must be done before the start of the submission period for your pathway; and

2   If you have any special needs or disabilities, RICS will, subject to notification and medical evidence, take appropriate measures to assist you at the assessment centre. There is a box on the application form to be completed if this is the case.

RICS will match panels and candidates in terms of background, training and experience, so that the detail of the interview may be correctly targeted by assessors with experience in similar areas to your own. If you need any help or advice regarding applying for final assessment, you can contact the RICS Contact Centre (see page 165).

Alternatively you can contact an APC doctor for advice on the final assessment requirements.

Final assessment interview

This book has been written in a logical order, that is to say, following the actual course of your APC. At first sight, therefore, it may appear that consideration of the final assessment interview at this juncture is a little premature. However, this is to give you an understanding of competency-based interviewing, so that you can start the mental preparation for the interview at an early stage. In particular, it is important that you are focused on this concept in the two to three month run-up period in which you will prepare your critical analysis and presentation.

Structured and planned revision and preparation for the final assessment will be critical. In many ways the final assessment can be compared to training for a major sporting event. To be successful, an athlete needs to approach the run-up to the big event in a planned and structured way, looking to peak, in performance terms, on the day. You will need to take the same approach to the run-up to your final assessment. Put the time and effort in, and you will be more likely to succeed.

In the lead-up to the big event, you need to have a clear understanding of competency-based interviewing, so that you can take an informed approach to the revision and preparation needed for the final assessment interview.

All good interviews essentially have eight important aspects:

1   they are objective;

2   they have set criteria;

3   the role of the chairman is clearly set out;

4   they have a defined structure identical for all interviewees;

5   they adopt a robust questioning technique;

6   note-taking is undertaken;

7   they provide equal opportunities; and

8   they are undertaken using professional conduct, best practice and with excellent customer care.

This chapter will look at the objectives and criteria in terms of how they link to competency-based interviewing; the remaining aspects of the interview will be discussed in chapter 5.

The objective

The objective of any interview must be clearly defined at the outset. Interviews are conducted for a variety of reasons – for employment, promotion, appraisal or dismissal.

The objective of the APC is to ensure that only those candidates who have an acceptable level of competence in carrying out the work of a professionally qualified surveyor on behalf of a client or an employer are admitted to professional membership of RICS – simply put, to test whether you are 'competent to practise' as a chartered surveyor.

Your competence will mainly be judged by the assessment panel asking questions, many of which will test your ability to put theory into practice. Throughout the interview, the assessors will set questions based on everyday problems faced by practising surveyors. This is an important concept. The APC is a *practical* test and assessment panels are made up of practising surveyors who are best placed to test your competence – based on their own up to date knowledge and current experience of the problems, issues and difficulties faced by the profession.

The criteria

In any interview situation, it is important that criteria are set. The criteria are the standards or benchmarks against which all candidates will be judged. They provide the consistency and uniformity required to create fairness, and equality of opportunity, for all candidates.

For the APC, the criteria or benchmarks are in essence the competency definitions of your selected pathway. During the training period you will focus on gaining experience which aligns with the levels in the various competencies and these will also be tested in the final assessment. It is this approach that will provide the fairness and level playing field for all candidates.

However there are also some developmental criteria, which have a longer-term connotation. Management is a good example, as management skills and abilities, if nurtured and developed, evolve over a period of time, whereas certain aspects of technical development can occur more immediately.

With regard to the developmental criteria, you will be expected to demonstrate that you have developed so that you:

- are a good ambassador for your profession, RICS and your employer;

- are aware of the professional and commercial implications of your work;

- understand your clients' and employer's thinking and objectives; and

- have an up to date and developing knowledge of legal and technical matters relevant to the work that you do and the law of the region or country in which you practise.

These criteria overarch the whole assessment process. If you think of the objective – becoming competent to practise – as a mission statement, the competency definitions and developmental criteria can be seen as the detail that underpin that statement.

Additional criteria have been set for the critical analysis and the presentation, which will be discussed both in this chapter (the critical analysis on page 96) and chapter 5 (the presentation on page 112).

A competency-based interview

The interview for the final assessment is largely competency-based. The objective of this is to allow you to demonstrate your skills and abilities against the various competencies and levels you have achieved during your training period. Whereas in a criterion-based interview the interviewer would mainly focus on knowledge and skills, in a competency-based interview, they will also consider attitude and behaviours. The philosophy behind the competency-based interview is that past behaviour is the best predictor of future behaviour.

Bearing in mind that the objective of the APC is to consider whether you are competent to practise as a chartered surveyor in the widest sense, the assessors will test knowledge of a range of issues of general relevance to your competencies and your pathway, as well as seeking to ascertain your awareness of your limitations and your knowledge of matters of wider concern to the profession. On occasions, therefore, you may be asked questions outside of your actual training and experience. A good example of this relates to the Rules of Conduct – the senior partner or managing director of your firm will usually deal with many aspects of the Rules of Conduct, such as managing client accounts, and in normal circumstances you will not gain hands-on experience of such matters, but you will still be expected to have some knowledge of the basic issues.

The assessors may also wish to test your ability to take learning and experience in one area within a competency or a number of competencies and apply it elsewhere. In other words, they may test skills transfer – stepping outside of your actual training and experience to ask you to apply what you have learnt to a hypothetical situation.

The objective, competencies and developmental criteria will be drawn together by the assessment panel during the course of the interview. The panel will take a competency and start by testing against the levels shown in the definition and include some of the developmental criteria, with a view to addressing the objective of the interview: Are you competent to practise as a chartered surveyor? For an example, see figure 6.

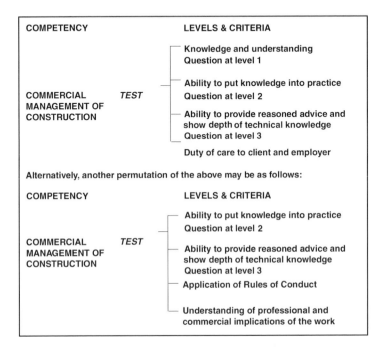

Figure 6 Questioning for competence in the quantity surveying and construction pathway

The aim of the assessment will be to test that you have attained the full range of competence required by your pathway. You will not necessarily be questioned in the interview against every competency. The evidence provided in your final assessment submissions will be used by the assessment panel in addition to the testing that takes place during the final assessment. Testing in one area may also draw upon evidence to support other competencies and criteria. As shown in the example above, the panel will do this by taking any of the appropriate competencies and asking questions to ensure that you meet the levels and criteria that have been set.

In the example of figure 6, the test of your ability to put theory into practice will also serve to demonstrate your knowledge of legal and technical matters, your awareness of the professional and commercial implications of your work and so on. Generally, you will find that in the course of testing your ability to apply your knowledge and understanding, an experienced assessor will draw out details of your knowledge, skills and abilities in relation to a large number of other competencies and criteria.

At the end of the interview the assessment panel will make a judgment about whether you have demonstrated the required level of competence. On this basis you will then be considered for professional membership of RICS, as the overall objective of the APC will have been met.

It is also important to note that in a 60 minute interview the panel will not be able to test everything you have learned in two years of training and experience. They will need to be selective – so don't worry if there are gaps and omissions in their questions – they may have been satisfied by some other piece of evidence or in the written submissions. Remember that it is not all down to questions and answers in the interview.

Now that you understand the basic concepts of the interview, you will realise that you will need to revise a range of issues that are of general relevance to your competencies, your pathway and to the profession. Below are some examples of when the panel interviewer may step outside of your actual training and experience in their questioning:

- Rules of Conduct – although you may not have hands on experience in all elements of the Rules of Conduct (perhaps particularly those for firms) the panel will expect you to have knowledge of the Rules of Conduct and of their implications on the practice of surveyors and their firms.

- Politics and economics – you should be aware of the general economy and the affect this has on property and construction.

- Taxation – although you may not have taken a specific competency in taxation you should be aware of general taxes and their impact on property and construction.

Other areas will depend on your pathway and chosen competencies. You should discuss this with your supervisor and counsellor as they will be able to guide you towards issues that are relevant to your pathway. APC doctors can also provide help in this area.

These examples should provide some guidance for the background reading you will need to do in preparation for the interview. You should put together a timetabled action plan for your revision that sets out the background reading and research you will need to do and identifies the sources of information you will use.

Final assessment submissions

The remainder of this chapter will consider your final assessment submissions, in particular the experience record and the critical analysis. You should refer to the guide for submitting your final assessment submission, available at www.rics.org/apc, for further advice on the submissions.

You will need to submit four copies of the Excel workbook for your chosen pathway, which includes all the necessary templates that you will have been using throughout your APC. The full set of templates to be submitted for final assessment are:

- Template 1 – candidate declaration – supervisors and counsellors will need to sign this template.

- Template 2 – candidate checklist.

- Template 3 – candidate achievement record – this must show compliance with the minimum number of recorded days needed and the achievement of the minimum competency requirements for the relevant pathway.

- Template 4 – professional development record – showing 48 hours of professional development for each year (see page 70).

- Template 5 – education record.

- Template 6 – experience record.

- Critical analysis.

You should also keep a copy of these templates for yourself. These same templates are submitted for all graduate routes (1, 2 and 3) and also for adaptation route candidates.

Experience record

The experience record was introduced on page 81 and will have been maintained throughout the course of your APC training. The objective of the experience record is to give the assessment panel details of the training and experience you have gained during the course of your APC. The information you provide should support the competencies and levels that you have achieved. Your record will give the panel practical examples of the work that you have been doing, to help them to properly target their questions to your training and experience. You should provide approximately 150–200 words for each level of competence you have achieved.

If you are a graduate route 3 or adaptation route candidate you will need to select your pathway and your optional competencies and prepare the experience record (or similar document) relating to your previous experience. You will also need to ask your sponsor to confirm that you have satisfied the competency requirements for your pathway, after which you must complete the candidate achievement record (log book summary element). You do not need to complete the log book or the number of days experience you have in the log book summary. Further guidance for graduate route 3 and adaptation route candidates can be obtained from www.rics.org/joinrics

Critical analysis

The critical analysis is a written report of a maximum 3,000 words. It is a detailed analysis of a project with which you have been extensively involved during your training period, with a conclusion giving a critical appraisal of the project, together with a reflective analysis of the experience gained.

The choice of project is very important as this forms a central component of the APC final assessment. Your role within an instruction or project that is considerable in size or importance could be an appropriate topic for the critical analysis but equally a small, low value project in which you had a very hands on involvement may be a suitable topic. The project that you choose need not be particularly complicated, or of great financial value; it may simply be typical of the type of work with which you have been involved.

It must be emphasised that you are not expected to be running the project you choose. It is your involvement or role in the team that you are expected to outline, analyse and comment on. It is also not necessary that the project has a definite start and finish point – it may be that at the time of writing your critical analysis the project has not reached a conclusion, so your report will comprise the detail up to the date of writing, and perhaps a prognosis of the outcomes.

The report may be supported by appendices. However, it is quality not quantity that is important, so do not include too many, or too lengthy, appendices. Appendices may be included to support your report but not to add or expand upon it.

The format of the critical analysis is clearly set out in the APC guidance and it is important that this is followed.

One of the main reasons for referral is that the guidance has not been followed and that the format of the critical analysis is too similar to the type of report that you would write at work. The main headings of the report should be:

- key issues;

- options;

- your proposed solution; and

- conclusion and analysis of experience gained.

The assessors are also looking for good communication skills, so think about the layout of the report, the presentation and use of photographs and plans, the grammar, spelling, number of words, index, pagination, and so on. This is an excellent opportunity for the panel to assess your written presentation skills.

As the assessors are also looking for a high level of professional and technical skills, make sure that this aspect of your report is checked and double-checked.

Main report headings in detail

Key issues

The project that you have been involved in could be fairly extensive. If you select too many key issues, it is likely that you will merely skim the surface of them, rather than undertaking a detailed analysis. So be selective – you may wish to select just one key issue. To meet the requirement of a 'detailed analysis' your commentary should address level 3 criteria for each of the competencies involved. This will provide the depth of analysis you are seeking.

Options and reasons for rejecting solutions

It is uncertainty that creates the need for experts, and it is the diversity of solutions to any particular problem that leads clients to request professional advice. Therefore, before proposing a solution to a client, you will need to consider all of the options. Under this heading, you must demonstrate your ability to think laterally and must show that you have genuinely considered other options to your preferred solution. Give reasons as to why some solutions were not feasible.

Do not fall into the trap of going down one route only. The APC guidance clearly requests that you consider a variety of options and give reasons why each one was rejected or selected.

Your proposed solution

You must give a detailed account of the reasons supporting your adopted course of action. Here again it is important that your thoughts cover a broad canvas. Too many critical analyses simply deal with the technical aspects of a particular job. Think about all the aspects that support your decision: financial, technical and professional, and issues relating to customer care, the Rules of Conduct, ethics and conflicts of interest.

Conclusion and analysis of experience gained

The conclusion of your report must include a critical appraisal of the outcomes, together with your own views and feelings about what you have learnt from the experience. This part of your report may account for between a quarter and a third of the total number of words.

The critical appraisal should be entirely introspective. All good professionals need to be able to look at a project, consider what they have done well, identify what they have not done so well, and plan how they might improve upon their actions the next time they carry out a similar task. This will make up your critical appraisal of the project. It is very important that your role within the project is absolutely clear to the panel and you should write the report in the first person.

The next step is to stand back from the project and reflect upon what you have learnt from the experience.

The assessors will take your critical appraisal as a starting point to question you beyond what you actually did and to probe your understanding of the wider issues surrounding your project. It is useful to start thinking about these aspects while you are writing your critical analysis and make additional notes to help you, rather than waiting until the interview.

You, your supervisor and your counsellor should provide a written declaration that the critical analysis is a true and accurate representation of your involvement in the project.

You must also ensure that you have your employer's and any client's consent to disclose any sensitive information in your critical analysis. If you are unable to obtain this then you should disguise any facts that might allow the panel to identify your project and you should make a note that this has been done. All information in your critical analysis will be treated in the strictest confidence by the panel.

Report writing

Writing repors is a key skill both within the surveying profession and specifically for the APC. The ten-point plan, set out below, will help you to write your critical analysis.

1 *The objective of the report*: never lose sight of it! In the critical analysis, you are looking to write a detailed analysis of a project (or projects) that you have been involved in during your training period. The conclusion to this report involves a critical appraisal of the outcomes, together with a reflective analysis of the experience gained. Keep this in mind throughout;

2 *Brainstorm the subject*: brainstorming is a simple technique where you take a topic or subject and write notes, in no particular order, of all of the thoughts and considerations that come to mind;

3 *Prepare an outline and consider the appendices*: start to put your brainstorming into some order, using

headings and important issues. Then consider the appendices that will be useful to support or shed light on the critical analysis. Do not fall into the trap of using the appendices to add to the volume of words; it is quality, not quantity, that the assessors will be looking for;

4 *Consider the use of visual aids, plans and photographs*: photographs can speak a thousand words and will be remembered by the panel. Remember that you will need hard copies of the visual aids for the interview;

5 *Stand back and review where you have got to*: are you still on course to meet your objective? Does everything look interesting and entertaining? How would you view the content if you were on the assessment panel?

6 *Write the report out in full*: start pulling the detail together, in terms of the text and appendices, plans, photographs, and so on;

7 *Once again review the report*: look at the number of words and check your spelling, punctuation and grammar very carefully;

8 *Polish the report*: design an attractive cover page and create an index. Number your paragraphs for easy referencing;

9 *Test the report for potential areas of questioning*: don't forget, the panel will be extending their questioning beyond what you actually did, and will also probe your understanding of any wider issues surrounding the project. It might be useful to ask one or two of your colleagues to read your critical analysis, with a view to asking you some test questions;

10 *Think about the objective once again*: has it been met? Go back to where you started and consider the following:

(a) have the key issues been made clear?

(b) have you considered the options and, in particular, the reasons for rejecting certain options/solutions?

(c) is the proposed solution supported by detailed reasoning?

(d) does the conclusion include a critical appraisal of the outcome and a reflective analysis of the experience gained?

The critical analysis is not an examination and you will have access to texts, references and a whole host of technical and professional references when writing it. It is therefore important to narrow down the key issues, so that you can write to the appropriate level of detail. In doing this, take care to ensure that the technical and professional references are to a high standard, as this will be an important issue for the assessment panel.

In summary, the criteria the assessors will be looking to apply to the critical analysis section of your assessment are:

● Has a suitable project been chosen?

● Have the key issues been identified?

● Have all the options been considered?

● Are the reasons for rejection of other options clearly stated?

● Is the preferred solution supported by sound judgment?

● Does the conclusion contain a critical appraisal and a reflective analysis of the experience?

● Has the candidate demonstrated high standards of presentation including spelling and grammar?

● Does the report indicate high standards of technical and professional skills and problem solving?

You will recall that earlier in this chapter the criteria that 'overarch' the final assessment process were considered. The above criteria clearly set out what the assessors will be additionally looking for in the critical analysis. Figure 7 shows the mark sheet used by the assessors when assessing your critical analysis.

Critical Analysis Title	Notes
Suitable project(s)/process selected for the critical analysis	☐ Met ☐ Not met
Key issues identified	☐ Met ☐ Not met
All relevant options have been considered and reasons given for those options which have been rejected	☐ Met ☐ Not met
Clear explanation of and reasons given supporting proposed solution	☐ Met ☐ Not met
Conclusion and critical appraisal of the proposed solution and outcomes	☐ Met ☐ Not met
Analysis of experience gained, demonstrating the candidate's learning and development	☐ Met ☐ Not met

A good display of professional and technical knowledge and problem solving abilities	☐ Met ☐ Not met
Overall standard of: • written presentation • layout • spelling • grammar • graphics	☐ Met ☐ Not met

Figure 7 APC assessor mark sheet – critical analysis

Summary

- You will have decided your target final assessment date with your supervisor and counsellor at the beginning of your APC.

- To apply for final assessment: send your application to RICS during the dates shown on www.rics.org/apc. You will then have one month to complete and send in your final assessment submissions.

- Make sure that you follow the guidance about applying available on www.rics.org/apc

- You must advise RICS of any special needs or requirements for the final assessment interview.

- The final assessment interview is mainly competency-based, but you should not lose sight of wider issues that impact on the work of surveyors within your professional group.

- Always stay clearly focused on the objective of the interview and on how the competencies and criteria fit together.

- The experience record is an important document, as it will help the assessors to target questions and lines of inquiry. Give plenty of examples of your work and make sure they are a true and accurate reflection of what you have been doing during the training period.

- Ensure that the format of your critical analysis complies with the guidelines set by RICS.

- Ensure that the critical analysis addresses the key issues of the project you have selected and gives reasoned support for your chosen solution or proposal.

- Give proper consideration to the critical appraisal and reflective analysis that is required in the conclusion to the critical analysis.

- Spelling, grammar, presentation and a demonstration of a high standard of technical and professional skills are also very important aspects of the critical analysis.

- Most importantly, ensure that your critical analysis meets the criteria that the panel will apply when assessing you.

The interview
and presentation

This chapter sets out the standard components of the final assessment interview. It seeks to expand and develop your knowledge and awareness of the role of the interviewer, and in so doing, to develop your technique as an interviewee. The presentation is also considered in detail.

Components of the interview

Your final assessment interview will contain a number of standard components. After the welcome by the chairman, your first task will be to give your presentation to the panel. The panel will then question you on the issues raised. Afterwards, they will question you on your wider training and experience, in relation to your chosen competencies.

Overview of the interview

The interview can be described as an information-gathering process in which the interviewer's most important skill is their questioning technique. You will do the majority of the talking. At the end of the interview, the assessment panel will consider the information gathered and how well it meets the criteria set for the interview. This, in turn, will determine whether the objective has been met, which will then determine whether you have been successful.

In chapter 4 we examined the various aspects of the interview, concentrating in particular on the objective and the criteria. This chapter will consider the other aspects in more detail:

- role of the chairman;

- structure of the interview (including the presentation);

- questioning technique;

- note-taking;

- equal opportunities; and

- conduct, best practice and customer care.

Under each section, an explanation of how the panel will operate is provided, followed by guidance on how you can improve and enhance your technique, with a view to delivering an effective performance, i.e. a performance that persuades the panel that you are 'competent to practise'.

You should appreciate that every interview you face will be different. In the context of the APC, no two assessment panels will operate in exactly the same manner. Therefore, the information that follows is provided in the context of guidance only, but hopefully it will be helpful for you.

Role of the chairman

The chairman of the assessment panel has a very important role to play during the interview – particularly with regard to the various aspects of the chairman's performance that are aimed at assisting you. The chairman will have made contact with the other panel members shortly after receiving your detailed information and final submissions from RICS. They will have held a brief discussion with the panel members concerning various aspects of the interview and will usually have arranged to meet them before the first interview.

A critical part of the interview is the opening three to four minutes. During this period the chairman's conduct will be geared towards settling your nerves. The final assessment interview can be considered as an 'advanced role play situation'. Consequently, you will probably be more nervous than you would be in a job interview. You could argue that there is much more resting on the outcome of this interview, given the years of effort you will have put in! with many more years of effort having gone into the preparation and this being the only 'job' in town! Therefore, the importance of settling your nerves and 'breaking the ice' is vital.

Figure 8 is a simple stress management graph that explains this concept in more detail.

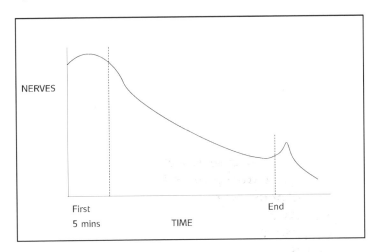

Figure 8 Stress levels during the final assessment interview

At the outset of the interview your nerves will be high. The chairman and panel members will aim to help you settle these nerves. Just before the end of the interview, when the chairman signals the close, your nerves will rise again for one last time. Your nerves may also increase somewhat as the interview progresses and you move from one panel member to another.

So how will the panel try to help you settle your nerves? There are a number of things they can do, such as:

- *introductions*: as soon as you enter the room, the panel will shake hands and introduce themselves, they may give you some relevant background information;

- *structure*: the chairman will generally give a brief outline of the structure of the interview. This will give you an idea of how the panel intends to organise the time and will help you to know what will happen next;

- *comfort*: the panel will make you feel comfortable by offering you a seat, water, the opportunity to take your jacket off, and so on.

- *notes*: the chairman will explain that the panel may be keeping notes. Do not be put off, therefore, if you see the panel scribbling away furiously. This is to assist with your assessment at the end of the interview;

- *health check*: after you have settled in, and before you move on to the presentation, the chairman may check to ensure that you are 'fit and well and ready to proceed' – or words to that effect. This check is to ensure that all candidates are given equality of opportunity. If you feel unwell before the interview, it is important that you do not proceed. You should tell the chairman, who will advise you what to do;

- *the ice-breaker*: the opening question asked by the chairman will be designed to 'break the ice'. The only way that you can get rid of nerves in an interview is by talking them out! The chairman will ensure that your first question is easy to answer and may be phrased something along the lines of, 'Tell us what sort of work you have been involved in over the last three months [or other period]'. Make sure that you are prepared for this question. Practise your response in advance, as this will help you at the beginning of the interview, when your nerves will be at a peak;

- *last word*: the panel will always let you have the last word. The chairman will say something like, 'At the end of the interview I will give you the opportunity to come back on, add to or clarify anything that we have discussed'.

The chairman may also keep you briefed at each stage of events, even though the structure has been outlined at the outset. This will help you to keep calm and is designed to give the interview some sense of continuity. The chairman may use phrases such as, 'Thank you for your presentation, we are now going to discuss some aspects of it with you. My colleague ... will begin'.

Your role

There are a number of ways that you can help yourself prior to the interview:

- Make sure that you know where the assessment centre is. Time your journey to give yourself plenty of time. Try not to put pressure on yourself by worrying about these things on the day – sort them out beforehand;

- If you have had any problems with the journey, or are unwell on the day, let the RICS staff know. This can be taken into account during the interview;

- Look the part. There is no doubt that a good first impression will give you a mental boost and will help with your nerves and confidence; and

- Rehearse your opening lines and prepare for the ice-breaker.

First impressions

Figure 9 shows how we let first impressions, which are often made in the first few seconds of meeting someone, form our views and opinions.

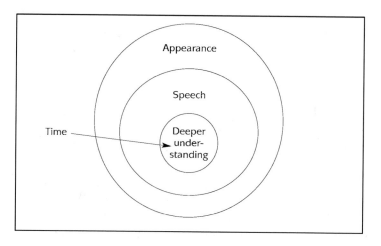

Figure 9 First impressions

When we meet someone for the first time, our initial impressions will be based on such things as stature, dress, and deportment. When the person speaks, they add to the mental picture we are building. We may immediately relate to the person's dress sense or accent, or may find that these do not conform with our 'norms'. We may therefore create a 'barrier', which can affect judgment and prejudice our views and opinions. It is only when we get beyond these first impressions that we really get to know someone and develop a deeper understanding of them.

The assessment panel will have been trained to deal with first impressions. To counterbalance the effect of such impressions, they will probably take notes during the interview, to ensure that you are judged on your overall performance, rather than initial impressions.

Structure of the interview

A well-structured interview has certain advantages. It will:

- provide order and discipline;
- help the panel cover the agenda – nothing will be missed;
- assist the panel with timekeeping; and
- provide a focus to proceedings.

You will probably find that the interview will start with a brief welcome and settling in period. The chairman will then ask you to give your presentation. This will be followed by approximately ten minutes of questions on the issues raised. Following this, the panel will move on to consider your wider areas of training and experience in relation to your chosen competencies, with the chairman and assessors taking it in turn to question you. This part of the interview may last for up to 35 minutes. The chairman will then spend a few minutes closing the interview and will give you the opportunity to have the last word.

Presentation

Your presentation will be based on your critical analysis. The objective of the presentation is to give the panel an outline of the purpose, investigations and conclusions concerning the work detailed in this report. It should last for ten minutes.

You should not simply read from a prepared speech. The panel will judge you on your personal communication and presentation skills, as well as on the content of the presentation itself.

You will be allowed either to sit or stand for your presentation. The panel will not, in normal circumstances, interrupt you during the ten minutes, although the chairman may let you know that you are approaching the end of your allotted time – indicating that you should begin to draw your presentation to a close.

You should note that presentation aids, such as overhead projectors and screens will not be available at the assessment centre. Laptops are not appropriate for this type of presentation – consider the use of flip charts that will fit on the table or perhaps just a short handout or simply some prompt cards for yourself. The presentation is more of a 'sit opposite and talk you through' than a 'stand and present to a large audience using IT' type of situation. And after all it is your personal presentation skills and your ability to communicate that are being assessed. After your presentation a ten-minute slot is allocated for questions relating to your critical analysis and to your presentation. The chairman may simply set the scene and then split the time 50:50 between the two panel members, or they may also wish to ask some questions, and will allocate time to do this.

TOP TIP

Consider your choice and use of visual aids carefully. If you use a handout make sure you refer to this in your presentation. If you use flip chart slides or prompt cards you might consider using ten, i.e. one per minute to help you to keep to time. If you use prompt cards you should attach these together to reduce the risk of dropping them on the day.

Criteria applied by the panel

A further series of criteria have been set to assess this part of the interview. During your presentation, you will be expected to demonstrate:

- good oral communication;

- presentation skills, i.e. eye contact, the appropriate use of body language, and voice projection, visual aids (if you use any); and

- clarity of thought (that is, your presentation should have a good structure).

Figure 10 shows the APC assessment panel mark sheet for the presentation.

Oral communication skills	☐ Met ☐ Not met
Clarity of thought and structure	☐ Met ☐ Not met
Presentation skills: • eye contact • body language • voice projection • visual aids (if any)	☐ Met ☐ Not met

Figure 10 APC assessment panel mark sheet – presentation

The mark sheet summarises how the panel will operate and what they are looking for. Consider the following when preparing for your presentation:

1 *preparation and rehearsal*: prepare, plan and rehearse. You might like to write your presentation out in full to learn from and then take prompts with you for use on the day. Rehearse in front of colleagues, family and friends. Ensure that the first time you give your presentation is not at your final assessment. You've got plenty of time to prepare, so make sure that you can deliver it backwards, standing on your head, in 9 minutes and 59 seconds!;

2   *structure*: think about the structure of your presentation and break it down into manageable chunks.

Consider the following five 'Ps':

- position: introduction – your name and outline of project;

- problem: key issues specific to the task;

- possibilities: lateral thought, options, why some options were rejected;

- proposal: option adopted, critical appraisal, lessons learnt and closing remarks; and

- preparation: forward plan before the day, and rehearse, rehearse, rehearse!

You will note that this structure fits neatly in with the structure of the critical analysis. By following this structure you should achieve the 'clarity of thought' criterion that the panel is looking for;

3   *make the presentation interesting*: you only have ten minutes, so do not laboriously repeat the details of a property, its construction, and so on. Get down to the problems and your solutions, i.e. the things that will interest the panel;

4   *the audience*: it is important that you consider your audience. Think about how you will manage proceedings, the possible use of a short handout, and so on and also remember that your audience are 'informed' – they do not need to know detailed general background that a practising surveyor would know anyway;

5   *key sentences*: use sign-posting at the beginning and end of each section of the presentation. For example, 'I would like to start by giving the panel a brief overview of my presentation' and 'That concludes my

opening remarks and I am now going to move on to the key issues and problems that I was faced with ...';

6 *pauses*: don't race through the presentation at high speed. Think about your pace and use pauses to denote the natural breaks in the structure and to signify the next chunk or section of your text;

7 *visual aids*: have a series of bullet points to jog your memory on a single sheet of paper or, if you need a little more, write the main headings with a series of bullet points underneath on postcards, which you can flick through during the presentation. You might also find a desktop flip chart useful. Using ten prompt cards (one for each minute) can be a useful way to keep to time – just remember to fasten the cards together in case of trembling hands on the day!;

8 *body language, voice and eye contact*: whether you sit or stand is a very personal decision. When making your decision whether to sit or stand bear in mind that the rooms are generally quite small and the panel will sit behind a table. You should, however, make this decision before arriving for your interview in order to save any indecision on the day. You should practise your presentation in advance in a similar situation to see how you will feel standing or sitting. Think of how you use your voice in terms of volume, pace and tone to emphasise issues or changes in direction. Eye contact is also important. If you are working from notes, make sure that you keep looking up and making eye contact with the chairman. Every once in a while let your eye contact 'sweep' the other assessors;

9 *make it personal*: speak in the first person and be very clear what your involvement was throughout the project.

10 **your appearance:** dress for success. Make sure that you feel confident as you walk through the door into the interview.

Questioning technique

Questioning technique is important in any interview. It is through questioning that the interviewer will gather the information needed to make a decision, based on the criteria, as to whether you pass the APC. It is important that you understand how the interviewer will operate and what techniques will be employed. Therefore this section provides an insight into the various skills that will be exercised by an interviewer.

During the course of the interview the assessors will mainly use open questions. An open question is generally where a sentence starts with the words: what, why, when, how, where or who. This allows you to expand upon your answers and provide the information that is required to assess your competence.

There may be occasions when the interviewer will use closed questions. A closed question will elicit a yes/no or one-word type of answer and will be used to clarify facts or information.

Assessors will ensure that questions are well-phrased, unambiguous and concise. They will usually ask one question at a time and use short scenarios and narratives to help you understand the question. Supplementary questions will be used to probe and test your problem-solving ability and depth of knowledge. They may also be used to help and encourage you in moments of difficulty.

Think in terms of three progressive levels of questioning:

- *level 1*: tests your knowledge and understanding of the theory behind any of the competencies;

- *level 2*: tests your knowledge and understanding in the context of the application of this theory to normal practical situations. Assessors will do this by targeting your training and experience;

- *level 3*: concerns your experience and ability to provide reasoned advice and reports to clients. There may also be reference to more advanced technical issues. This will be done with regard to your experience, but there may be elements of questioning at this level that are outside your direct training and experience. This is covered in more detail below.

As a general rule the assessors will ask you questions about your knowledge of a subject for level 1, questions about your past experience for level 2 and scenario-based questions for level 3.

As an example, the following is a typical line of questioning from the rural pathway. It is based on the agriculture competency (T002):

- 'I notice from your experience that you have carried out a rental valuation of Quarry Hill Farm. How did you go about the inspection, particularly in relation to the farm buildings, land and crops?' (level 1);

- 'In preparing your valuation, and over and above these physical factors, what part did budgets and profitability play? How did these matters affect your thinking and approach to the valuation?' (level 2);

- 'I note that your client in the situation was trading at a loss. What factors did you consider or look at before advising on how to proceed with changing the business in terms of crops grown, overheads, marketing and general management?' (level 3).

> An alternative approach to level 3 might test the provision of advice to the client:
>
> - 'What issues and headings did you cover in your valuation report to the client?'

Be aware that if you have achieved a competency (as assessed by your supervisor and counsellor) to level 1 or 2, the assessors' questioning will not probe beyond that point. However, don't forget you may be tested outside of your main areas of training and experience within and beyond some of your competencies.

The phrasing and approach to questions that are purely targeting an area of competency may be as follows:

- 'Give me an example of...'

- 'I see from your experience record that you have...'

- 'What was your role/involvement in...?'

- 'Outline the process/procedures that you employed/adopted...'

- 'What problems did you encounter...and how did you solve them...?' 'What was the outcome...?'

- 'What did you learn...?'

Problem solving and learning is a key feature of competency-based interviewing, so be prepared for this line of questioning.

The questions relating to 'stepping outside' of your experience may be phrased as follows:

- 'What would you do differently next time...?'

- 'How would you apply this experience in tackling...?'

- 'What if a situation/problem arose...?'

- 'You have not had specific experience of...so in theory how would you...?'

- 'Where might you seek further advice and guidance...?'

This approach is very much geared to the 'big picture' so far as the objective of the APC is concerned – assessing that you are 'competent to practise'. It looks to test skills transfer and to assess your ability to take learning and experience in one area of practice and apply it to another. In addition, it seeks to establish that you are aware of your limitations – hence the line of questioning concerning seeking further advice and guidance.

The above outlines the approach to questions relating to the core and optional competencies. You should also be aware of the approach that will be adopted to test the mandatory competencies.

Ordinarily, when testing mandatory competencies, the assessors will refer to your past experience, rather than adopting a theoretical, textbook approach. Because of time constraints in the final assessment interview, assessors have been advised to keep the time spent on these competencies in proportion. A large part of the interview will be devoted to the technical aspects of the core and optional competencies. You will find that very often the demonstration of your ability in the mandatory competencies will be woven into the main fabric of the interview, and will be drawn out of your responses to the technical questioning in your core and optional competencies, as well as from your written reports and presentation.

However, there will be occasions when you will face some specific questioning. A typical approach is for the panel to target the professional development that you have carried out in order to develop knowledge and understanding at level 1 in any of the mandatory competencies.

Some examples of questioning approaches are as follows:

- What procedures does your firm have in place to ensure the delivery of high quality client care? (level 1);

- From your experience of ... can you provide an example of how you have applied one of these principles? (level 2);

- What do you consider to be the key components of a good presentation (or negotiation)? (level 1);

- Give the panel an example of a recent negotiation, how did you prepare, what was the outcome? And how did you judge success? (level 2);

- What do you understand to be the key principles involved in successful teamworking? (level 1).

Figure 11 is a representation of the APC assessment panel mark sheet for the interview.

Attach the achievement record – log book dummary pages ONLY (template 3). Relate your marking to the competencies noted in template 3.		
	Notes
Mandatory competencies	☐ Met ☐ Not met
Technical core competencies	☐ Met ☐ Not met
Technical optional competencies	☐ Met ☐ Not met
Rules of Conduct/ethics	☐ Met ☐ Not met
Professional development	☐ Met ☐ Not met

Figure 11 APC assessment panel mark sheet – interview

Interviewee technique

A useful ten-point guide for you as an interviewee is:

1 *ice-breaker*: make sure that you prepare for the ice-breaker in advance. Give it some thought and use it to provide the panel with some further insight into your training and experience;

2 *pause for thought*: before responding to questions, always pause for thought. The panel will not be expecting you to leap into answers. Always stand back for a moment, consider the question, collect your thoughts and then deliver your response – look before you leap;

3 *active listening*: think of listening in an interview as an active skill, rather than a passive, skill, and make sure you concentrate on what is being said. In an examination, you would read a question and then read it again, to stimulate and recall information relevant to the subject. In an interview, you will usually have only one chance to hear the question, so practise repeating the words in your mind as it is being asked by the assessor. This will help you to commit the question to memory and assist your powers of recall when answering it;

4 *repeat the question*: if you are not entirely sure what the question was, ask the assessor to repeat it. This is a useful technique to employ if you are asked a long-winded and complicated question – it will force the assessor to revisit the phrasing of the question and may help to focus your thoughts. However, you should do this only sparingly;

5 *chronological order*: think about chronology when giving your response. A lot of the questions you will be asked will command a response with a natural chronological order, for example, relating to techniques employed or the order of carrying out a

123

particular task or function. This will help you to collect your thoughts and ensure that you do not miss any important aspects of the response required;

6 *key issues*: if there is no chronological order inherent in your response, you may prefer to think of your answer in terms of key issues or bullet points. In this respect, you may find it helpful to use the various competency statements as a guide to your preparation for the interview. These statements will provide the trigger for the areas of questioning by the panel;

7 *unfamiliar areas of experience*: in the interview you will be asked questions outside of your main areas of experience. In these instances, do not be afraid to qualify your response. Don't forget, the assessor may have placed you outside of your main areas of experience in order to test how well you can draw from these areas and apply your learning and knowledge to an unfamiliar territory. Make sure you qualify your answers by indicating whether you have only limited or no experience in any particular subject area;

8 *mental blocks*: everyone suffers from nerves during an interview situation. There may be occasions when you have a complete mental block or stumble with the answer. Don't worry, the panel are trained to help you in these situations, for instance, by giving you more time, or approaching a question from a different angle. You will also be offered the opportunity to return to areas of questioning at the end of the interview;

9 *bluffing*: do not try to bluff or waffle your way through any of the answers. The assessors will all be experienced surveyors and will probably detect when you are unsure or are attempting to guess the answers. Often, when we are unsure in an interview, our body language or tone of voice can be a

give-away. Bluffing will also give a bad impression in terms of duty of care and being aware of your limitations. If you are not sure of an issue, or really have no idea of the response required, simply tell the panel;

10 *final word*: you will be offered the last word by the chairman when the interview is drawing to a close. At this stage only reopen an area of questioning if it is absolutely vital. Close the interview by thanking the assessors for their time, smile and leave the room.

Note taking

The assessors may take brief notes during the interview, to ensure that they are being fair to candidates. Do not be unnerved by this. It is being done for your benefit, to ensure that the interview is a fair and impartial assessment of your performance.

The notes taken will, in the final analysis, assist assessors in considering whether to pass or refer you. In the event of a referral, the notes will be an invaluable source of information and guidance for you.

Equal opportunities

The need to be conscious of equal opportunities crops up in many aspects of the final assessment process. The main points are:

- the assessors will keep a record of the interview;

- the chairman will handle the opening five minutes with great care to help settle your nerves;

- the chairman will ensure that you are 'fit and well and ready to proceed'. They will check that you are not suffering from ill health;

- the chairman should control time across the interview as a whole and within the various components;

- the assessors will link questions to your training and experience in terms of the mandatory, core and optional competencies;

- questioning will mainly relate to the competencies and criteria set down for the APC; and

- the chairman will give you the last word before drawing the interview to a close.

Conduct, best practice and customer care

The panel will think of you as its 'customer' and consider 'best practice' to be about the delivery of excellent customer care. The preparation beforehand, the tone of voice used when asking questions and the way that the assessors look at you during the interview will all affect how you feel and therefore perform.

In an interview situation, these matters are important to both the interviewer and interviewee. Let us now consider some of these issues from both sides of the interview table:

- *room layout*: the chairman will ensure that the environment within which the interview takes place is prepared to your advantage. They will ensure, for example, that you will not be staring into the sun. The chairman will check that the panel have name cards in front of them so that you are not forced to remember names from the introductions. Before you enter the room, think about how you will greet the panel. As soon as you enter the room, decide where you will put your plans and papers;

- *eye contact*: you must always remain attentive and appear interested. However, do not spend the whole time 'eyeballing' the chairman or one of the assessors. Try to think about looking just over the interviewer's left shoulder, right shoulder or just below the chin. This will take the sting out of the eye contact, but will still signal to the panel that you are focused and attentive;

- *attentiveness*: sixty minutes is a long time to remain attentive. It is easy to gaze out of the window for a few minutes, read from some of the details in front of you, or fidget. Stay conscious of the impact that such actions may have on the panel;

- *body language*: you must be aware of the impact that body language can have on your performance. Be conscious of your facial expressions – a pained look may immediately convey the impression that you are finding an area of questioning difficult. Never underestimate the importance of a smile in terms of building a rapport with the panel. Also think about how you sit – avoid sitting with your arms folded, or leaning forward, eyeball to eyeball, and speaking in a harsh or agitated tone of voice. This will not give the panel a good opinion of you;

- *voice projection*: your tone needs to be warm and enthusing, the volume positive and confident and the pace such that the panel is able to follow and understand your answers;

- *listening skills*: your ability to listen and concentrate during the course of an interview is important to ensure that you interpret the interviewer's questions correctly; and to help you convey interest and attention through positive body language;

- *closing the interview*: before drawing the interview to a close, the chairman will ask if you have anything else to say. This opportunity will be kept within the parameters of the interview. The chairman might say, 'Is there anything we have discussed that you would like to add to or clarify?', thereby avoiding reopening the interview on an entirely new topic. After this, the chairman will probably say, 'The interview is now finished. Thank you for attending'. They will stand, perhaps give a final handshake, and gesture or lead you to the door. It is important that you leave on a positive note, so try to smile and don't forget to say thank you.

Summary

- An interview is an information-gathering process, with the aim of providing the interviewer with the information that will satisfy the objective of the interview.

- Rehearse your opening lines so that you get off to a good start. This will help with your nerves.

- Dress for success. If you look good, you will feel good.

- If you are unwell, advise the RICS staff at the assessment centre, who will provide you with any assistance required.

- Practise your presentation extensively before the day, so that you can deliver it with confidence.

- In discussion with your supervisor, counsellor or colleagues, try to anticipate the questions that may be asked about your presentation.

- Focus on the criteria that have been set for your presentation: good oral communication skills, presentation skills and clarity of thought.

- Understand the difference between open and closed questions and practise responses that make use of chronological order or summarise key points.

- Practise active listening.

- Use the competency statements and guidance on pathways while preparing and revising for the interview. These statements will act as the focal point for the questions from the panel.

- Do not be put off by the panel taking notes. This is for your benefit, to ensure that the final assessment is fair and is based upon the evidence presented by you.

- At the end of the interview always smile and thank the panel for their time.

Appraisal, referral and the appeal system

6

This chapter will consider what happens after the final assessment interview. It will look at how the assessment panel reaches their decision and will also consider referral reports and how you can make an appeal.

Candidate appraisal

After your interview the panel members will consider how the details of your training and experience have stood up to questioning during the interview.

As a starting point, they will consider your performance against the four broad headings that equate to the concept of being 'competent to practise' (see chapter 1):

1   core competencies;

2   optional competencies;

3   mandatory competencies; and

4   conduct rules, ethics and professional practice.

The assessors will link the mandatory, core and optional competencies to these four headings to arrive at their decision. There will, of course, be a great deal of overlap – for example, you will demonstrate your oral communication skills each time you answer a question. Figure 12 indicates the mental links the assessors will make between the competencies.

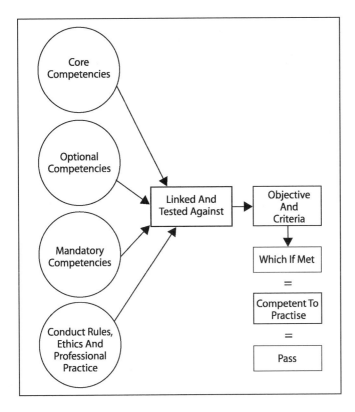

Figure 12 Candidate appraisal

It is, therefore, vital that you have a clear picture in your mind of what being 'competent to practise' looks like from the outset. Your goal should be to demonstrate these areas of skill and ability during your final assessment interview.

As well as questioning you on your training and experience, the panel will ensure that you meet the minimum training requirement of 400 days of experience gained within 23 calendar months (assuming you are a graduate route 1 candidate).

The panel will then move on and consider your critical analysis and presentation. These will be considered against the criteria set for these components of the final assessment (see chapters 4 and 5). Finally, they will consider your experience record. They will also check that your professional development meets with the minimum requirement of 48 hours per annum (taking account of any allowance for part-time or distance learning study – see page 70).

Drawing the components together – the holistic view

The panel will take a holistic view of your performance and then make a decision as to whether you are considered 'competent to practise'. All candidates are different and skills will vary. Some candidates will show strength in technical and professional matters and perhaps be a little weaker with interpersonal and communication skills. With other candidates, the opposite may apply.

Role of the chairman

During the decision-making period, the chairman will ensure that there is a consensus of opinion and will seek the panel's final view. They will listen to the panel members, particularly with regard to their areas of specialism, and will weigh and balance their views to ensure that the final decision is fair.

Final decision

Remember that you will not be expected to demonstrate a level of knowledge and experience equivalent to that of an experienced practitioner. The panel's decision will be based on you having demonstrated competence to the required level, tested against the various criteria that have been set. The panel will not be expecting a level of knowledge equal to that of their advanced years. The panel will wish to be confident that you are a 'safe pair of hands', that you are aware of and intend to act within the RICS Rules of Conduct, that you know your limitations and have a good, rounded knowledge and that you possess the necessary skills within your competency areas and in general areas of relevance to your pathway.

It is also worth noting that there are no quotas or pass rates for the APC. The benchmarks that the assessment panel will work to are the levels of competence required, tested against the various criteria set out in the APC guidance. All candidates that meet these requirements will pass the final assessment.

Results will be sent to you by first-class post within 21 days from the date of your interview. Remember to let RICS know if your correspondence address changes. A pass list will also be published on the RICS website after each assessment period. For security reasons, no results will be given over the telephone, by fax, email or to a third party.

Referral reports

In the event of a referral, the chairman of your assessment panel will provide you with as much information as possible. The panel will have been asked to give reasons as to why you did not meet the required levels of competence. These will be given with reference to the specific competency (mandatory and technical) and with a clear explanation of how you have fallen short of the criteria. You may also receive advice on further training and development that has been identified as suitable by the panel. You will also receive feedback on your professional development and on your critical analysis, presentation and interview. Finally, you may receive feedback on aspects of your performance that were satisfactory. The objective of this is to enable you to address any weaknesses before the next assessment and to be successful when you resit.

Receiving a referral report will be a miserable experience. However, you must remain positive and focused. Go back to some of the key concepts behind the critical analysis, be introspective, learn from your mistakes and improve areas of weakness. You have the benefit of the experience, so learn from it and build upon your strengths, to enable you to be successful on the next occasion. Be philosophical. It may be that you were not quite ready for the final assessment.

If you are referred, there are some minimum requirements that you must satisfy before you resit the final assessment. You must:

- record further professional experience. The assessors will probably give you guidance on this;

- address the deficiencies identified in the referral and get those competencies signed off again by your supervisior and counsellor.

- undertake a minimum of 24 hours more professional development;

- write a new critical analysis; or resubmit the original, if recommended, suitably amended and updated;

- submit a copy of your referral deficiency report and professional development deficiency record giving details of the further training and experience in relation to the competencies and professional development undertaken.

Appeals

If you are unsuccessful and are in any way aggrieved by any aspect of the final assessment, you can make an appeal. This must be received by RICS no later than ten days from the date on your results letter. The details of how and when to lodge an appeal will be sent with the referral report and application for reassessment. (These details can also be found on www.rics.org/apc)

If you do feel aggrieved immediately after the interview, consider the following points:

- it is very difficult to get a feel for the outcome of an interview immediately afterwards. Your nerves and adrenaline level will still be high and you will find it difficult to be truly objective;

- if you are still feeling aggrieved when you get home, sit down and write a list of the aspects of the interview that went well, and then make a list of the aspects that did not go well, noting why you feel unhappy;

- after 24 hours, go back to your notes and consider whether there are any aspects you still consider to be unfair.

When you receive the result, you may well be pleasantly surprised. So do not overreact to one or two aspects of the assessment that did not go so well. The tendency in a highly charged interview situation is to remember only the downsides.

Two examples of why an appeal may be made are:

- administrative or procedural matters: the panel may not have been provided with the correct information and detail; or something may have gone wrong, for example, denying you the opportunity to make your presentation; or

- the questioning and testing of competence concentrated too heavily outside of your main areas of training and experience.

Hopefully, such problems will not arise. In case they do, however, RICS has an established appeal system.

Appeal system

If you do want to make an appeal, it is important that it is made by you, and not a third party. You must make the appeal in writing, accompanied by the appropriate fee; and you need to clearly state the grounds on which the appeal is being made, supported by appropriate evidence.

Your appeal will be considered by an appeal panel made up of senior experienced assessors.

If your appeal is successful, your fee will be returned and a reassessment, using all of the original paperwork, will be arranged as soon as possible. You will be reassessed by a different panel and the normal rules and procedures will apply. Conversely, if your appeal is rejected, you will be eligible for reassessment along the lines of the notification that was sent with your referral report.

Advice and further guidance

- Be introspective and do some soul-searching. Is there anything you can learn from the referral to make you successful on the next occasion?

- With your referral report at hand, talk to your employer, your supervisor and your counsellor.

- You should also consider asking your employer to approach your RICS training adviser (RTA).

- You should consider contacting your local APC doctor for advice and assistance on preparing for reassessment.

- With your supervisor and counsellor, consider how additional professional development could assist you in addressing any of the shortcomings noted in your referral report.

Summary

- Ensure that your paperwork and final submissions are in order. The panel will check to ensure that you meet the training and experience requirements (a minimum of 400 days within 23 calendar months for graduate route 1), as well as the final assessment record and professional development requirements.

- In drawing the components of the final assessment together the panel will take a holistic view of your performance.

- The decision will be arrived at by considering the views and opinions of all panel members. This is to ensure a fair and balanced outcome.

- The panel will not be working to quotas or pass rates.

- If you are unhappy with the interview and wish to make an appeal, try to be objective. Seek advice from your supervisor and counsellor.

- If you wish to make an appeal, you must do so no later than ten days from the date on your results letter.

Conclusion

As we have discussed throughout this book the APC is foremost a period of training and practical experience. If you follow the guidance and ensure that you are learning the skills and reaching the levels of attainment required in the various competencies, you will be well on your way to a successful final assessment interview. If the training and experience has been correctly put in place over the required period leading up to the final assessment, the outcome should be a formality.

It is when candidates have not followed the various guidance available, and have not remained focused on the competency requirements, that the final assessment results in an unsatisfactory outcome.

It is also essential that you focus on the various skills required for the final assessment: report writing, presentation and interview skills. The practical guidance set out in the previous chapters should provide you with some insight to the challenges that lie ahead, not just with the APC, but for the rest of your career.

Finally, the following is a list of vital points to be borne in mind as you progress through the APC:

- Once you're accepted as an APC candidate, RICS will confirm your registration and give you a start date for recording your experience (RICS will allow you to back date your experience for up to a month provided you have been employed by your current employer for that time – contact the Membership Operations department for more detail (see page 165));

- if you change employer during the training period, you must inform RICS;

- the training period is a minimum of 400 days within 23 calendar months for graduate route 1, or 200 days within 11 calendar months for graduate route 2;

- professional development must comprise a minimum of 48 hours per annum;

- you must have achieved the appropriate number of competencies, and to the levels required by your pathway, before you are eligible for the final assessment;

- the final assessment is mainly a competency-based interview, but be prepared for questions outside of your main areas of training and experience. Remember, you are being interviewed to test whether you are 'competent to practise' overall as a chartered surveyor;

- stay focused on the competency statements for your pathway, particularly the criteria that overarch the assessment, as well as those that apply specifically to the critical analysis and presentation; and

- throughout your APC remember that there is a wide range of help and support available for you and for your employer, including:
  - your supervisor and counsellor;
  - APC doctors;
  - RICS training advisers;
  - the APC team in the RICS Membership Operations department;

- the RICS website;
- RICS Books;
- RICS Matrics;
- the RICS library; and
- other APC candidates.

One final point is that your learning and development never ends. Your professional competence will continue to be assessed by employers, clients and peer groups throughout your career. As the world around you changes in terms of consumer demands, law and technology, the content and focus of your learning and development will also change.

Therefore, when you become chartered, think of your lifelong learning or CPD as a vehicle to assist you with your essential and ongoing training and development needs, in a rapidly changing environment.

Frequently asked questions

Answers to some questions that are often asked of RICS training advisers, APC doctors and in the APC discussion forum.

Enrolling and employment

See chapter 1 for more details.

I have more than 10 years experience and am a member of another professional body. Is there a route to membership without further study?

If your membership is an approved professional qualification for graduate route 3 (a full list of approved qualifications can be obtained from the RICS website), then, asssuming that your experience is considered relevant you can apply to go straight forward to the APC final assessment. You should submit a resume of your experience to the RICS Contact Centre in the first instance. A resume template is available on the RICS website and details of the final assessment are also available on the website or from the Contact Centre.

Note: Graduate route option 3 is also available for candidates with 10 years experience and an RICS-accredited degree. The adaptation route is also available for candidates who hold a surveying related non-accredited degree, have nine years or more experience and who are willing to convert their existing degree by an adding an additional 450 study hours from the final year of an RICS accredited degree.

I enrolled for my APC a few years ago and have let things lapse including my diary record! What can I do to get back on track?

You may be eligible to transfer to a different APC route that will allow you to fast track to final assessment. If you have more than five years' experience you may be able to transfer to graduate route 2 and undertake one year of structured training and the final assessment. If you have more than ten years' experience you may be able to transfer to graduate route 3 and go directly forward to final assessment. Full details can be obtained from the RICS website or from the RICS Contact Centre.

What can I do about my APC if I am made redundant or leave my job?

If for any reason you leave your job you should ask your supervisor and counsellor to have a final meeting with you and to confirm your competency achievements and to ensure that all the necessary documentation is up to date before you leave.

If you do find yourself unable to reach the competency levels you need for your APC pathway either due to redundancy or the fact that your work is very limited due to current economic circumstances, consider the following:

- Remember that you do not have to be in paid work to be gaining experience for your APC. Working on a voluntary basis is just as valuable.

- If you need to change your pathway due to change in work you should advise RICS via the Contact Centre,

download the Excel workbook for your new pathway
and cut and paste any relevant experience into your
new competency selections in your experience record
and other templates.

- If you need to change your competencies due to a
  change in your work:

  - You should update your log book with the new
    competencies and begin to record your
    experience against these both in your diary and
    in your experience record.

  - If you are very close to completing the required
    number of days and your supervisor and
    counsellor have confirmed you have met the
    minimum competency requirements for your
    pathway it may be possible for your employer
    to put forward a case to RICS for being unable
    to complete further training due to the current
    economic climate. Consideration will then be
    given to exercising support and flexibility.

- Under extreme circumstances, it may be possible for
  simulated experience to be used to gain competencies.
  Your employer will need to gain consent for this
  though before putting anything in place.

- If you feel you are not going to be able to achieve the
  necessary competencies for a while but have made
  good progress you might consider applying for
  Associate membership. It is likely that with a
  surveying degree and at least a year of structured
  training you would be close to satisfying the
  requirements for this membership.

- If you wish to defer your final assessment this can be
  done but you should advise RICS at apc@rics.org.

If you are made redundant and are within two months of
achieving your full diary experience you should contact

the RICS Contact Centre as it may still be possible for you to go forward to final assessment.

If you have gained your full experience and have achieved the necessary competencies but are made redundant you may still be able to submit a critical analysis on a project you worked on with your previous employer. If it is not possible to gain permission from the company you may be able to avoid mentioning confidential matters and explain the situation to the assessment panel.

There are concessions available on RICS membership fees and possibly refunds of APC fees if you are not continuing. The RICS Contact Centre can give further advice on this.

LionHeart, an independent charity run by RICS members, have issued a useful guidance note on redundancy. This can be obtained from www.lionheart.org.uk

Finally if you have any queries about how changes in your work affect your APC you should discuss this with an APC doctor.

Structured training agreements

See page 72 for more details.

What is a structured training agreement?

The purpose and status of the structured training agreement (STA) is to help the employer in the efficient development of APC candidates. A separate structured training programme should be devised for each candidate but this does not have to be separately approved by RICS. The structured training agreement is an agreement between your employer and RICS stating their intended policy for implementing the requirements of the APC.

RICS approval of this document grants the employer accredited employer status. It is up to your employer to update the structured training agreement in the light of changes to work practices or changes to RICS requirements. The STA is also a statement of how the employer intends to implement the requirements of the APC process and is an agreement from the employer to comply with this process as detailed in the APC guidance and in accordance with the RICS Rules of Conduct. Draft structured training agreements should be submitted to RICS for approval.

For further advice and assistance regarding the development of structured training agreements or structured training programmes you should contact the RICS training adviser for your area.

How can I find out whether my employer has an approved structured training agreement?

All organisations for which a structured training agreement has been approved are listed on the RICS website.

What should I do if my employer does not have an approved structured training agreement?

Firstly, ask your employer to take a look at the official APC guidance, which provides information relating to the structured training agreement. They could also look at the book *Supervisors and Counsellors Guide to the APC* which provides information relating to the Structured Training Agreement. You can also download a template for the agreement from the RICS website. The agreement does not have to be in this form but your employer may find this a useful starting point.

Your local RICS training adviser would also be very happy to come in to see you and your employer to provide advice regarding the development of a structured training agreement.

The structured training agreement must be in place and approved before you can enrol for the APC.

Experience records

See page 81 for more details.

How much detail should I put into my experience record template?

You should write up to 200 words for each level of each competency you achieve. You should use this to summarise the entries in your diary and to give the assessment panel information regarding your experience over your entire APC journey. Details should include real life examples of projects, processes and procedures that you have dealt with. These should be named where possible but if there are confidentiality issues then you can just explain the broad nature of the project. You should refer to the official APC guidance when writing this to ensure that your record shows compliance with the competency levels you are achieving. You should also refer to the pathway guides to gain an understanding of the areas of work with which the APC panel would expect you to be involved at each level of each competency.

I am taking graduate route 2 for candidates with 5 years or more experience. Do I need to maintain a diary of my experience for the period of 11 months structured work experience?

Yes, you must keep a diary as you will be asked to submit a log book and experience record with your final assessment documentation. The log book will indicate how many days you have spent in each competency area during the 11 months.

Should I record time in my APC diary against the mandatory competencies?

No, you should only record time against your core and optional competencies.

Professional development

See page 70 for more details.

How do I allocate my professional development activity between the technical, personal and professional categories required?

The official APC guidance indicates the required 48 hours per year of professional development be allocated between these three categories with a minimum of 16 hours in each category. The Excel workbook templates require you to allocate each of your listed activities to one of these categories.

Professional development relating to your technical competencies (i.e. your core and chosen optional competencies or possibly any wider subjects you have covered) should be categorised as 'technical'.

Professional development relating to your mandatory competencies (other than professional ethics and practice) should be categorised as 'personal'.

Professional development relating to the professional ethics and practice competencies should be categorised as 'professional'. This might include structured reading about the RICS Rules of Conduct for example.

I am studying on a two year part-time/distance learning RICS accredited degree while undertaking my APC. Can this be used towards the professional development requirement?

The final year of your course can be counted towards your professional development requirement for that year.

However, you should supplement this with additional professional development activity.

What can I include as professional development activities?

There are a very wide range of activities that can be included as professional development. You should, however, try to ensure that at least one third of your professional development is a formal activity (i.e. not private study/reading). The crucial point to remember though is that you must be able to demonstrate that you have learnt from the activity and that it is relevant to your role as a surveyor, to your pathway and to your competencies.

The following are some examples of activities that could be included as professional development:

- Professional work-based activities, for example work-based research, team meetings, professional discussions with colleagues, team briefings.

- Personal and informal learning, for example structured reading, web-based research, DVDs, podcasts, use of *isurv*.

- Courses, seminars and conferences. These need not be only RICS events and it may be that you would also include professional networking around the main event as well.

- Voluntary or charity work. This need not necessarily be property work but activities that help you to develop transferable skills such as communication, team working and leadership.

Professional development need not be certificated but you must evaluate each activity and show how it has helped you to maintain or enhance your competence as a surveyor.

Critical analysis

See page 96 for more details.

How should I choose a project for my critical analysis?

The choice of project is very important as your APC assessment panel will review the appropriateness of your choice as part of their assessment. You should be confident that the following is true of your project:

- It is a real life project that you have been closely involved with during your APC period (or prior to that if you are taking graduate route 3 or the adaptation route).

- It focuses on some of your core competencies and ideally some mandatory and optional competencies as well.

- It is relevant to your chosen APC pathway.

- It gives you the opportunity to appraise different options or courses of action.

- You find the project interesting (this will come across to the panel and will help you to give a good presentation).

- You are able to access information that you may need to present your project.

- You feel comfortable with the issues raised in the project and will be able to respond to questions from the panel regarding these.

The project need not be of great value or size – it is your involvement that is important and it is this that the panel wish to hear about.

Assessment

See chapter 4 for more details.

I have heard mention of an interim assessment. Do I need to undertake an interim assessment for my APC?

No, the requirement to undertake a formal interim assessment was removed some years ago. You should note, however, that the experience record must be completed at each supervisor and counsellor review and your supervisor and counsellor should use the 12-month review (for graduate route 1 candidates) to assess progress more generally and to review your structured training agreement and competency achievement planner and make any adjustments necessary.

Finding help

What is an APC doctor?

APC doctors are members who offer pathway-specific advice and guidance to APC candidates. Their advice, usually provided by email or telephone, can include:

- how to enrol;
- how to record experience;
- completion of the necessary templates;
- choice of project for the critical analysis;
- format for final assessment written submissions;
- application for final assessment;
- the final assessment interview;
- key issues of interest to your professional group (i.e. areas of possible questioning at interview); and much more.

APC doctors are not able to comment on actual draft submissions for final assessment but can provide advice on the general approach.

Queries relating to training, competency planning, structured training agreements and programmes, assessment of competencies, experience limitations and supervisor or counsellor queries should be directed to RICS training advisers.

A full list of APC doctors and contact details for the doctor looking after your APC pathway are available from the RICS website.

Who can help me?

There are many people who can help you with your APC. These include:

RICS training advisers

They work as part-time consultants for RICS. Their role is to provide support and advice for employers of APC candidates. RICS training advisers will be happy to arrange to visit you and your employer at your office to discuss your training, your APC competencies and to work with your employer to set up and operate a structured training agreement. They can provide advice on the most appropriate route and pathway through the APC, on what your employer needs to do to meet the requirements at any stage of the APC and also provide advice on the final assessment.

Your APC supervisor

Your supervisor should generally be your immediate manager and will know your work well. The supervisor need not necessarily be a member of RICS but must, of course, be experienced in your area of work. Your supervisor will work closely with you through your APC, helping you with choosing and achieving your competencies, meeting the requirements and assessing your competence every three months, recording this in your achievement record. Your supervisor will also help you in preparing for the final assessment and in choosing a suitable project for your critical analysis.

Your APC counsellor

The role of your APC counsellor is a strategic one focussing on your planning and training programme and monitoring your performance against your chosen competencies and pathway. Your counsellor must be a chartered surveyor, preferably from the same organisation as yourself but could also be from outside the organisation so long as your supervisor is happy with this. Your counsellor will again help you in choosing and achieving your competencies and will assess your competence every six months, recording this in your achievement record. Your counsellor will also work with your supervisor to give you advice and guidance in preparing for your final assessment.

APC doctor

APC doctors work with RICS training advisers to provide a local independent point of contact for you to discuss your experience and to give assistance in preparing the various APC documentation and in preparing for final assessment. The APC doctors are volunteers and are all practising chartered surveyors. You can find contact details on the RICS website.

RICS Membership Operations

The RICS Membership Operations Team in Coventry are available to help with general enquiries regarding your APC and issues such as timings for final assessment submissions and other APC administration queries you may have. They can be contacted via the RICS Contact Centre on 0870 333 1600. The Contact Centre staff are also able to deal with many queries relating to APC administration.

Other APC candidates

Getting together with other APC candidates can be a great way to share ideas and experiences. It can be beneficial to start a self-help group and meet up to discuss your diaries, log books and supervisors in an informal setting. Also, consider getting involved with your local Matrics group for APC support and networking. Visit www.rics.org/matrics

APC timeline

The following timeline represents the minimum amount of time required to reach final assessent on graduate routes 1 and 2.

Stage	Month for graduate route: 1	2	Actions
Structured training agreement	0	0	• Ensure structured training agreement is approved. • Supervisor and counsellor to be appointed.
APC enrolment	1	1	• Send in enrolment form and payment to RICS. • Commence diary recording. • Complete diary, log book and professional development record.
Complete templates	2		• Complete diary, log book and professional development record.
Supervisor's assessment	3		• Complete diary, log book and experience record. • Attend supervisor assessment and complete candidate achievement record.
Complete templates	4 and 5		• Complete diary, log book and professional development record.
Supervisor's and counsellor's assessment	6		• Complete diary, log book and experience record. • Attend supervisor assessment and complete candidate achievement record.
Complete templates	7 and 8		• Complete diary, log book and professional development record.

Supervisor's assessment	9		• Complete diary, log book and experience record. • Attend supervisor assessment and complete candidate achievement record.
Complete templates	10 and 11		• Complete diary, log book and professional development record.
Supervisor's and counsellor's assessment	12		• Complete diary, log book and experience record. • Attend supervisor assessment and complete candidate achievement record. • Begin to identify suitable projects for critical analysis.
Complete templates	13 and 14	1 and 2	• Complete diary, log book and professional development record.
Supervisor's assessment	15	3	• Complete diary, log book and experience record. • Attend supervisor assessment and complete candidate achievement record. • Identify and agree critical analysis project.
Complete templates	16 and 17	4 and 5	• Complete diary, log book and professional development record.
Supervisor's and counsellor's assessment	18	6	• Complete diary, log book and experience record. • Attend supervisor assessment and complete candidate achievement record.
Complete templates	19 and 20	7 and 8	• Complete diary, log book and professional development record.

Supervisor's assessment	21	9	• Complete diary, log book and experience record. • Attend supervisor assessment and complete candidate achievement record. • Review final draft of critical analysis.
APC final assessment application (must be within set dates; see RICS website)	22	10	• Review APC with supervisor and counsellor. • Finalise critical analysis and all templates. • Ensure all competencies have been achieved (or will be in the next month). • Apply for final assessment.
APC submissions	23	11	• Ensure all your templates are finalised and all signatures have been provided. • Send in final assessment submissions.
Final assessment	24	12	• Attend final assessment.
Results	25	13	

Index

RICS contact details and further information

There are numerous ways of contacing RICS and a wealth of information sources online for APC candidates.

RICS Contact Centre

T: +44 (0)870 333 1600

F: +44 (0)20 7334 3811

E: apc@rics.org

RICS website

The RICS website provides details on the routes to membership, how to enrol and how to apply for the final assessment. You can also download the APC guidance, templates, Excel workbooks and pathway guidance and find your nearest regional training adviser and APC doctor. Visit www.rics.org/apc

RICS Books

T: +44 (0)870 333 1600

F: +44 (0)20 7334 3851

E: mailorder@rics.org

www.ricsbooks.com

isurv

isurv is an online knowledge resource for property professionals, brought to you by RICS. The *isurv* 'channels' cover a huge range of surveying topics, mixing expert commentary with official RICS guidance. Visit www.isurv.com

The *isurv* APC channel also holds excellent support material and provides links to information relevant to achieving each competency. Visit www.isurv.com/apc